William S. Bur

Titles in the series Critical Lives present the work of leading cultural figures of the modern period. Each book explores the life of the artist, writer, philosopher or architect in question and relates it to their major works.

In the same series

Jean Genet
Stephen Barber

Michel Foucault
David Macey

Pablo Picasso
Mary Ann Caws

Franz Kafka
Sander L. Gilman

Guy Debord
Andy Merrifield

Marcel Duchamp
Caroline Cros

James Joyce
Andrew Gibson

Frank Lloyd Wright
Robert McCarter

Jean-Paul Sartre
Andrew Leak

Noam Chomsky
Wolfgang B. Sperlich

Jorge Luis Borges
Jason Wilson

Erik Satie
Mary E. Davis

Georges Bataille
Stuart Kendall

Ludwig Wittgenstein
Edward Kanterian

Octavio Paz
Nick Caistor

Walter Benjamin
Esther Leslie

Charles Baudelaire
Rosemary Lloyd

Jean Cocteau
James S. Williams

Sergei Eisenstein
Mike O'Mahony

Salvador Dalí
Mary Ann Caws

Simone de Beauvoir
Ursula Tidd

Edgar Allan Poe
Kevin J. Hayes

Samuel Beckett
Andrew Gibson

Pablo Neruda
Dominic Moran

Vladimir Nabokov
Barbara Wyllie

Constantin Brancusi
Sanda Miller

Gertrude Stein
Lucy Daniel

William S. Burroughs

Phil Baker

REAKTION BOOKS

Published by Reaktion Books Ltd
33 Great Sutton Street
London EC1V ODX, UK
www.reaktionbooks.co.uk

First published 2010

Printed and bound in Great Britain
by Cromwell Press Group, Trowbridge, Wiltshire

British Library Cataloguing in Publication Data
Baker, Phil, 1961–
    William S. Burroughs. – (Critical lives)
    1. Burroughs, William S., 1914–1997.
    2. Authors, American – 20th century – Biography.
    3. Beat generation.
    I. Title II. Series
    813.5'4-DC22

ISBN 978 1 86189 663 6

Contents

Haunted: a preoccupied Burroughs in Duke Street, London, photographed by Jim Pennington, 1972.

1

St Louis Blues

Looking back on childhood in his autobiographical novel *Junky*, Burroughs wrote that he could put down 'one of those nostalgic routines' with the old German doctor next door, the rats in the backyard, and his pet toad that lived by the pond. But instead, he says, his earliest memories were marked by anxiety: fear of the dark, fear of being alone, fear of nightmares where a 'supernatural horror' seemed always on the verge of taking shape and breaking through into waking life. It was through these nightmares that he was already attracted as a child – at least within his own telling, his personal myth – to the idea of opium. Hearing a maid talk about it, and how smoking it brought sweet dreams, he said 'I will smoke opium when I grow up.'[1]

William Seward Burroughs II was born on 5 February 1914 at 4664 Berlin Avenue, St Louis, Missouri, a pleasant, tree-lined road which changed its name to Pershing Avenue during the First World War. It was a three-storey brick house with a large garden and a pond at the back, well suited to people like Mortimer and Laura Lee Burroughs; people with middle-class tastes who were comfortably off but not wealthy. Young William was named after his grandfather, the William Seward Burroughs who invented the famous Burroughs adding machine. He had rescued the project from initial disaster, when it was found that the machines gave different figures depending on how hard the handle was pulled. The banks sent them back and Burroughs faced ruin, but then he discovered the pull could be regulated by a hydraulic oil device, and the machine was in business again. As his namesake wrote in *Naked Lunch*: 'no matter how you jerk the handle result is always the same for given co-ordinates. Got my training early . . . wouldn't you?'[2]

On his mother's side Bill was descended from a staunch Southern Methodist preacher, James Wideman Lee from Georgia, and perhaps more distantly related to Confederate General Robert E. Lee (a widespread claim among Southerners named Lee). Laura Lee's brother Ivy updated the family's rhetorical background as a pioneer in the nascent art of Public Relations. Known as 'Poison Ivy' Lee, he was at the top of his profession, with a client list that included the Rockefellers. In the 1930s, IG Farben – the German firm now remembered for manufacturing Zyklon B, the gas used in the Holocaust – paid him to improve Hitler's image in America.

Another uncle, Horace Burroughs, became a morphine addict. He was one of many, back in the years of America's 'Dark Paradise'[3] of legal opiates, which only came to an end in the year Bill was born, with the 1914 Harrison Narcotics Act. 'Has anyone considered the simple fact,' Burroughs asked in an interview, 'that drugs were legal in America until somewhere around 1914? You could buy morphine, heroin, cocaine, all sorts of tinctures, extracts of cannabis . . . Good for man and beast . . . Yessir, the good old days . . . They don't even like to admit the 19th century existed, that there was a time when drugs could be sold in America.'[4] Horace Burroughs killed himself in 1915 at the age of 29.

Grandfather Burroughs overworked, drank hard, and died from TB in his early forties, leaving his business partner Joe Boyer to make a fortune and change the company name from the American Arithmometer Company to the Burroughs Adding Machine Company. The Burroughs family were not as rich as they are sometimes said to have been, and although Mortimer Burroughs sold his stock shortly before the Wall Street Crash, it was only worth $200,000. Mortimer Burroughs ran a plate-glass business, then went into landscape gardening, and finally he

Gracious living: Laura Lee Burroughs's 1940 book on flower arranging.

Flower Arranging – A Fascinating Hobby

by Laura Lee Burroughs

and his wife ran a gift shop named Cobble Stone Gardens ('lawn furniture, yard ornaments, barbecue sets, small bric-a-brac of various kinds . . . they did pretty well'[5]).

With the gift shop and the landscape gardening, both parents had aesthetic interests; Laura Lee was also a noted flower arranger, and later wrote three weirdly atmospheric books on 'Refreshing Arrangements', sponsored by the Coca-Cola Corporation. 'Mexico – the land of flowers, color, and life in a pleasant tempo – was the inspiration for this table', she says: 'The madonna under the shelter of a tin candelabra, the plates, chairs, glasses, vases, mirror and the incredible fruit banks all came from Mexico.' Of another, 'Low Price Glamour', she writes: 'This whole set-up is a triumph of mind over finances. The candelabra was purchased from an iron shop for a small sum . . . We point with pride to the soda fountain chairs gilded and upholstered, looking adorable . . .'[6]

Mrs Burroughs was an attractive, gracious woman, although 'crippled by her Bible Belt upbringing, which had imposed an abhorrence of bodily functions.'[7] As if to compensate, she was psychic, or so it seemed to her son: 'My mother . . . had a dream that my brother Mort came in with blood running down his face and he said "Mother, I've had an accident." Actually, at that very moment, he *had* had a car accident and cut his face up.'[8]

For all Laura Lee Burroughs's attempts at gracious living, the Burroughses were not quite out of the top drawer, and they knew it. They were in the St Louis Social Register but not the St Louis Golf and Country Club. Grandmother Burroughs was in the Colonial Dames but not the Daughters of the Revolution. They were invited to parties, but only big parties. As Burroughs put it, 'no one wanted those ratty Burroughses about'.[9]

Still, $200,000 was a solid sum, and the modest family fortune ran to several staff: a cook, a maid, a gardener, a butler, and a nanny or nurse. The cook and nurse were both superstitious women and put frightening supernatural ideas into William's head. The old Irish cook taught him how to 'call the toads', apparently bringing out the toad that lived by the fishpond, and she also taught him a curse about a blinding worm. This involved a piece of mouldy bread and a needle, and a rhyme that ran

> Needle in thread, needle in bread
> Eye in needle, needle in eye
> Bury the bread deep in a sty.[10]

His nurse, Mary Evans, was Welsh and she had an old Welsh curse:

> Trip and stumble
> Slip and fall
> Down the stairs
> And hit the wall.[11]

There was something more about Mary Evans, but Burroughs never knew what it was. During his years of psychoanalysis he could never recapture what happened, but it seems to have been abuse of some kind at the hands of Mary and her boyfriend. Burroughs's most graphic treatment of the incident is in a 1950s text called 'Word', where he suggests that as an infant he bit the boyfriend's penis in self-defence. In a slightly later conjecture, arising from analysis, he thought he had witnessed Mary's illegal abortion and the subsequent burning of the foetus.[12]

Ted Morgan pictures the exasperated psychoanalyst saying 'What is this that has affected you your whole life?'[13] and Burroughs never quite knew. In 'Lee's Journals' he writes of Mary the nurse:

> The memory he could never reoccupy, even under deep narco-analysis. Whenever he got close to it, excitation tore through him, suppressed below the level of emotional coloring, a neutral energy like electricity. The memory itself never actually seen or re-experienced, only delineated by refusals, disgusts, negation.[14]

Whatever it was, it must have contributed to a lifelong sense of being internally undone, or always already impinged on.

Mary Evans left the family employment suddenly, perhaps under a cloud. But there were happier moments. Burroughs remembered walking every day to Forest Park with his brother and nanny, who would tell them 'Don't ask questions and don't pass remarks'.[15] Forest Park had a pagoda left over from the 1904 St Louis World Fair (as in the song, 'Meet me in St Louis Louie / Meet me at the Fair . . .') and there was a funfair attached with roller coasters, a Ferris wheel and a penny arcade, later to be a motif in his work. Burroughs remembered 'hot peep shows in the penny arcade'.[16]

St Louis was a mixed place. It was deep in the Midwest, almost a frontier town, with a vein of no-nonsense Missouri pragmatism and scepticism (it was the so-called 'Show Me State', where the inhabitants believed nothing but their own eyes; '*I know what I have seen,*' Burroughs once wrote in a letter, '*being strictly from*

Forest Park, St Louis, where Burroughs was taken by his nanny: the alligator pond.

Missouri"[17]). Then it had a strong strain of gentility about it, and was the world of the young T. S. Eliot, a writer with whom Burroughs has affinities. The mother of the boy next door on Pershing Avenue, Rives Skinker Matthews, had been to dancing classes with young Tommy Eliot and remembered his socks would never stay up.

And then it had a more unsavoury side, which Burroughs particularly savoured. Along with fond memories of sitting on the back porch on summer nights drinking Whistle (a sugary soft drink; the advert ran, 'He-boys drink it through a straw'), he remembered the ashpits at the bottom of the garden and the River des Peres just beyond, which smelt of coal gas and was virtually an open sewer. In a later work entitled *Cobble Stone Gardens* he brings his trademark crazed hyperbole to imagining the St Louis citizens complaining 'My teenage daughters is cunt deep in shit. Is this the American way of life?'

'I thought so,' says Burroughs, 'and I didn't want it changed.'[18] Then there was the red light district of East St Louis, 'a marginal district of vacant lots, decaying billboards and cracked sidewalks where weeds grow through the cracks.'[19] Market Street was a long way from the gentility elsewhere in St Louis, a place where you might see a knuckleduster in a pawn shop window, 'the skid row of my adolescent years . . . tattoo parlors, novelty stores, hock shops.'[20] There was a museum of venereal horrors – once a widespread cautionary attraction, with gruesome and disturbing waxworks – with its seedy barker outside: 'This museum shows all kinds social disease and self-abuse', he would cry, and 'Young boys need it special'[21] – an utterance later to be another motif in Burroughs.

Burroughs's first school was the local Community School. He was not popular, particularly with parents and adults. He looked like a sheep-killing dog, said one, and another thought he was like a walking corpse.[22] Sixty years later Burroughs would drawl to the audience in packed readings 'It's not every corpse that can walk . . . hers can't.'[23] Revisiting his childhood in the persona of Audrey Carson, he writes 'Audrey was a thin pale boy, his face scarred by festering spiritual wounds.'[24]

In 1925 Burroughs joined the John Burroughs School (named after a famous naturalist; no relation) shortly after the family moved to the suburb of Ladue, where Mortimer Burroughs built himself a house in five acres of ground on South Price Road. Burroughs was still not well liked, but here he made a lifelong friend in Kells Elvins, a handsome, athletic, popular boy. In later years they would collaborate on writing together and see each other all over the world, from Mexico to Denmark to Tangier.

For now Bill adored Kells, who would sometimes put Bill on his lap and strum on him like a banjo, which Bill found sexually arousing. Kells was resolutely heterosexual and very successful with girls and later women, despite a streak of misogyny that led him to belittle them and treat them badly. 'They'd cry on my shoulder', Burroughs remembered, 'and I'd say 'I'm sorry, but if you want to put up with it then that's your concern.'[25]

Young Burroughs was fond of guns and weapons, and he experimented with home-made explosives. His father had first taken him duck-shooting at the age of eight, and when the family went on holiday to France he bought himself a sword cane and a cane gun. A schoolmate, Ann Russe, remembered Burroughs sitting at the back of the class and aiming his Eversharp propelling pencil at other pupils like a gun. Sometimes she would feel an odd prickling sensation in her scalp and turn around to see Bill was aiming it at her.[26]

Bill's brother Mort got on naturally well with his father, but Bill didn't, although they tried. 'My father was a strange man. He puttered around in the basement making these pirate treasure boxes. He was a skilled craftsman. I had a .22 rifle once that I wanted to convert into a pistol and he fixed it up with a pistol grip.'[27] Instead Bill was very much his mother's son, and she adored him to a point that was almost embarrassing.

Bill wasn't a strong child and he had sinus trouble, so in the hope of improving his health and toughening him up it was decided to send him to the Los Alamos Ranch School in New Mexico. High up on the mesa overlooking the Rio Grande, it was a select and expensive school with an outdoors, Boy Scouty ethos. The school song ran:

Far away and high on the mesa's crest,
Here's the life that all of us love the best –
Los Alamos![28]

It was later taken over as the site of the American atom bomb tests, an irony that weighed heavily on the adult Burroughs. He hated the Bomb and thought it should never have been used on Japan.

Burroughs was not happy at Los Alamos: he disliked the horse riding and the cold and the values of the place – where reading was actively discouraged because it was for sissies – although he liked

Young Burroughs at Los Alamos Ranch School, c. 1930.

fishing and hiking, enjoyed the rifle range, and had a role in a school play as a pistol-packing character called 'The Toff'. He also became a proficient knife thrower. Whether from quiet desperation or simply in search of kicks, it was at Los Alamos that he overdosed on chloral hydrate, a well-known 'knockout drop' of the day. It ended badly, but it was Burroughs's first experiment with drugs. The school director, A. J. Connell, had to write to Bill's parents to tell them what had happened, and he reassured them, 'I doubt if he will try anything like it again.'[29]

A. J. Connell was a peculiar man, and in some respects Los Alamos – although it was a good school in its way, and very successful in turning out future captains of industry – was a peculiar place under his leadership. Connell, a former scoutmaster, was a gun-toting Forest Ranger who had previously worked as a decorator or perhaps window dresser of some kind for Tiffany's in New York. There was nothing fake about his tough outdoorsmanship, but at the same time his room had 'so much magenta damask . . . it looked like the madam's parlor in a bordello.'[30]

A. J. loved his boys and the Los Alamos regime was one of barely repressed homosexuality. A. J. liked to measure the boys regularly, without their clothes, and to burst in on people – there were no door locks – to check they weren't masturbating. He knew Burroughs's parents slightly, and one day he was alone with Bill in their house when he suddenly told him to strip naked, and questioned him: did he play with himself, and did he do anything with other boys?

Bill's time at Los Alamos was overshadowed by an unhappy obsession with another boy there, who rejected him and told the others about him, making him a figure of fun or worse. Burroughs confided his feelings of unrequited love at great length into his diary. He was in misery, and his mother wrote to A. J. Connell to say his letters had been 'very blue and depressed'.[31] Bill was within a couple of months of graduating from Los Alamos and A. J. Connell didn't want him to leave, but his mother took him away, using foot trouble as an excuse, and he made his escape so fast he left his belongings behind, including the diary.

Burroughs then suffered further miseries back in St Louis, as he imagined the boys reading his diary aloud to each other. Eventually his trunk arrived, and he found the now hateful diary was still hidden and intact. Looking at it again, he was horrified by the triteness of his feelings, as well as the risk of showing them. Later there would be a regular strand of savagely ironized romantic sentimentality in his work: 'a silo full of queer corn'[32] as he would call it.

A. J. must have been disappointed by Bill's departure, and the school's final report described Burroughs as intelligent but lacking in direction and 'morbid and abnormal'.[33] Bill told his mother he was queer, and she sent him to the first of his many psychiatrists, a Dr Schwab, who gave them some reassuring words about the Greeks, and growing out of it.

All this time, before the debacle of the diary, Burroughs had been writing. Despite the Los Alamos line on reading, he still read 'more than was usual for an American boy at that time and place: Oscar Wilde, Baudelaire, Anatole France, even Gide.'[34] He combined these with a steady diet of pulp fiction from publications like *Amazing Stories*, and altogether it gave him a sense of the mystique of writing:

> As a young child I wanted to be a writer because writers were rich and famous. They lounged around Singapore and Rangoon smoking opium in a yellow pongee silk suit. They sniffed cocaine in Mayfair and they penetrated forbidden swamps with a faithful native boy and lived in the native quarter of Tangier smoking hashish and languidly caressing a pet gazelle.[35]

Burroughs's first attempt at writing came when he was eight. He wrote 'The Autobiography of a Wolf', inspired by Ernest Seton Thompson's *Biography of a Grizzly Bear*. People would say to him, 'You mean biography of a wolf.' 'No,' said Burroughs, in another line he would drawl out at readings in old age, 'I meant the *auto-biography* of a wolf, *and I still do*.'[36]

There was a vein of sentimentality and self-sacrifice in Burroughs's earliest writing, where Audrey the wolf dies after losing his wolf mate Jerry. A few years later, English polar explorer Lord Cheshire gives the last of his lime juice to his team mate Reggie as they are dying on the ice floe, and bravely lies about it ("Have you had yours?' . . . 'Yes,' said Lord Cheshire, 'I've had mine.'). Sentimental self-sacrifice comes back in the later stories 'The Junky's Christmas' and 'The Priest, They Called Him', where the protagonist gives his last shot of junk to a neighbouring boy in physical pain, then dies, receiving 'the *immaculate fix*.'[37]

Then 'There was something called *Carl Cranbury in Egypt* that never got off the ground . . . Carl Cranbury frozen back there on the paper, his hand an inch from his blue steel automatic . . . I also wrote westerns, gangster stories, and haunted houses'.[38] Hanging was the method of capital punishment in Missouri, and it featured in the newspapers and in Burroughs's stories, particularly the Westerns: 'Hardened old sinner that he was he still experienced a shudder as he looked back at the three bodies twisting on ropes, etched against the beautiful red sunset.'[39]

Burroughs's first published piece of writing appeared in the school paper, the *John Burroughs Review* of February 1929, when he was fourteen. It was entitled 'Personal Magnetism' and detailed his experience of replying to an advertisement. 'Are you bashful? Shy? Nervous? Embarrassed?' said the ad. 'If so, send me two dollars and I will show you how to control others at a glance . . .'.[40] Burroughs was none of these things, he said, but he still wanted to control others at a glance, especially his Latin teacher Mr Baker. He clipped the coupon, 'beginning to feel more magnetic every minute', but unfortunately the book that arrived was 'a mass of scientific drivel'. Burroughs did find out how to control people

but never had the nerve to try it. Here is how it is done: I must look my victim squarely in the eye, say in a low, severe voice 'I am talking and you must listen,' then, intensify my gaze and say, 'You cannot escape me.' My victim completely subdued, I was to say, 'I am stronger than my enemies.' Get thee behind me Satan. Imagine me trying that on Mr Baker!

I think the book was right in saying that by following its instructions I could make myself the center of interest at every party. Interest is putting it mildly!

Young in style and keen to befriend the reader, 'Personal Magnetism' is sane, funny and unfooled. More than that, it is a prescient piece not just for its interest in control but for its voyaging into a 'small ad' world of psychological jiu-jitsu and shortcuts to psychic mastery. Burroughs would later become absorbed in Scientology, and he never quite lost contact with sub-standard, mail-order style intellectual sources: even the title concept of his celebrated collaboration with his friend Brion Gysin, *The Third Mind*, comes from Napoleon Hill's 1937 *Think and Grow Rich*.

Burroughs encountered the book that was to have the greatest effect on his writing when he was about thirteen. This was the autobiography of a criminal, Jack Black's 1925 *You Can't Win*, which catches the reader's attention right from the dedication

> . . . to the unnamed friend who sawed me out of the San Francisco jail and to that dirty, drunken, disreputable, crippled beggar, 'Sticks' Sullivan, who picked the buckshot out of my back – under the bridge – at Baraboo, Wisconsin.[41]

'Stultified and confined by middle-class St Louis mores,' Burroughs writes, 'I was fascinated by this glimpse of an underworld of seedy rooming-houses, pool parlors, cat houses and opium dens'.[42] Jack Black becomes an opium addict (a 'hop head' or 'dope fiend' in the language of the day) before finally managing to quit, and the book's straightforward, informative memoir style was a model for Burroughs's *Junky*:

> Given a sufficient quantity of hop, no fiend is ever at a loss for a sound reason for taking a jolt of it. If he is feeling bad he takes a jolt so he will feel good. If he is feeling good, he takes a jolt to make him feel better, and if he is feeling neither very bad nor very good he takes a jolt 'just to get himself straightened around.'[43]

In the pages of Jack Black Burroughs met honourable criminals like the Sanctimonious Kid and Salt Chunk Mary, the hard but fair fence who always kept a pot of coffee and some pork and beans on the stove for guests. He could remember scenes and characters fifty years later, incorporating them into his own work ('I felt a deep nostalgia for a way of life that is gone forever . . .').

Above all he met the Johnson Family, an association of 'good bums and thieves . . . a Johnson pays his debts and keeps his word. He minds his own business, but will give help when help is needed and asked for.' Of Sticks Sullivan, the beggar who picked the shot out of the author's back, Burroughs says simply: 'Sticks was a Johnson.' As time went by the Johnson became central to Burroughs's vision of a divided world, with a 'basic split' between Johnsons and Shits:

> Looking back over the years, I remember the Johnsons . . . the old Mexican druggist who filled a morphine Rx [prescription] after ten shits had snarled it back at me: 'We do not serve dope fiends!' Yes, I remember the old Johnsons; and I remember those of another persuasion. As a wise old black faggot said to me, 'some people are shits, darling.'
> *And likely to remain so.*[44]

Like the disease museum and the penny-arcade peepshows, Jack Black and his Johnsons always stayed with Burroughs.

2

The Hidden Antagonist

'The environment was empty, the antagonist hidden',[1] Burroughs
wrote of his early life, and a general sense of malaise and exclusion
continued to hang over him as he proceeded to Harvard in 1932 to
study English Literature. Late in life he reproached Ted Morgan for
describing him as a literary outlaw, saying he had never had any
base in law to reject or leave.[2] A sense not of being an outlaw but
a simple outsider dominated his existence.

At Harvard he was in an unfashionable House, Adams House,
he failed to join any clubs, and he hung out in an odd and slightly
seedy little set that included an Irishman who claimed to be related
to royalty, a lordly Englishman, and another friend who became
intractably schizophrenic in his early twenties.

Burroughs received a good education at Harvard. He attended
George Lyman Kittredge's then famous Shakespeare lectures, learned
a great deal of Shakespeare by heart, and took a course on Coleridge's
imagination with John Livingston Lowes, author of the classic study
The Road to Xanadu. He also saw T. S. Eliot give one of his Charles
Eliot Norton lectures. At weekends Burroughs would sometimes go
with a friend to New York, where he visited nightclubs in Harlem, and
it was at one of these that the 'wise old black faggot' remembered in
the Jack Black introduction (a man named Clinton Moore, who ran
a club) let him into the open secret that some people are shits.

Burroughs had read a short story by H. H. Munro, or Saki, in
Saki's 1912 collection *The Chronicles of Clovis* which seems to have

made an impression on him. It was about a polecat-ferret named Sredni Vashtar and a sickly little boy named Conradin, who lives under the matriarchal hand of his guardian, Mrs De Ropp, whom Saki calls 'the Woman'.[3] She is the model on which Conradin 'based and detested all respectability', while Sredni Vashtar is his 'god' and 'idol'. When Mrs De Ropp decides to get rid of the boy's beloved pet, Conradin prays to Sredni Vashtar for help, and Sredni Vashtar kills her. And now, at Harvard, Burroughs kept a ferret in his room called Sredni Vashtar.

He also kept a gun in his room, against regulations, and narrowly escaped a lethal accident when he went to fire what he thought was the empty gun at a friend and put a bullet in the wall. With his gun and his ferret, Burroughs didn't go unnoticed, and he was disliked by his housemaster, James Phinney Baxter.

Burroughs's friends were astonished when he let slip that he thought babies were born through the navel; a popular sexual theory of children, but unusual in Harvard undergraduates. At St Louis during the long vacation (where he had a job as a cub reporter on the *St Louis Post Despatch* and hated it, being sent to 'doorstep' bereaved parents for photos of their tragic offspring) he started going regularly to a brothel, where he always had the same girl. Back at Harvard, he had sex with a young man from the town and caught venereal disease.

Burroughs left Harvard in 1936 with a BA in English, syphilis and $200 a month from his parents as a graduation present. This wasn't the Burroughs 'trust fund' – a myth spread by Jack Kerouac – but it was about $3,000 a month at today's values, and it made a difference. Burroughs's parents also sent him to Europe after graduation, where he and a friend saw Paris, Vienna, Budapest and Dubrovnik. In Budapest they met Baron Yanchi Wolfner, the model for Von Pregnitz in Christopher Isherwood's *Mr Norris Changes Trains*. He was a key player on the queer scene there, with his monocle and what Burroughs remembered as a 'sort of English public school veneer'.[4] In Dubrovnik they met a Jewish woman named Ilse Klapper, a rather Weimar Republic-looking character who also wore a monocle. She had a sense of humour and Burroughs liked her.

Burroughs decided to stay on in Europe and study medicine in Vienna. Later in life he could reminisce with Isherwood and Tennessee Williams about the Romanische Baden, the old Roman baths and the Prater amusement park with its Ferris wheel (as in *The Third Man*) but his time in Vienna was not very happy. It was overshadowed by having syphilis and discovering he didn't like studying medicine, with its vast burden of facts to be memorized.

To cap it all he developed appendicitis in spring 1937 and needed an emergency operation, after which he went back to Dubrovnik to convalesce and met Ilse Klapper again. She wanted to get out of Europe to escape the Nazis, so Burroughs married her. She was about fifteen years older, which caused some raising of eyebrows, but it was a sucessful ploy. They never lived together but they later saw each other as friends in New York, until she went back to Europe after the War.

Having returned to St Louis from Vienna, his medical career over before it had started, Burroughs was still at a loose end and searching for something unknown. He enrolled to do graduate study in psychology at Columbia but found it was a sterile subject dominated by statistics. Then he found his old friend Kells Elvins had gone to Harvard, where he was doing a Master's degree in psychology, so Burroughs followed him there in 1938.

Elvins was already married but separated, and he and Burroughs shared a house with a black servant to do the cleaning and cooking. Burroughs studied Mayan archaeology, and the Mayans became a lifelong interest; exoticism in Burroughs is often pre-Columbian rather than Asian, including human sacrifices and the mysterious obscenity of Chimu pottery. In particular, Burroughs became fascinated by the way that the Mayan priest class were able to dominate the people ('In the Mayan culture the priests were only

Frederick Catherwood's picture of a Mayan altar, formerly thought to show Ah Pook, Mayan god of death.

one percent of the population. They had no police force, and no army, so they must have had some very effective means of psychic control.'[5]). It seemed to be because every aspect of life was intrinsically controlled by the Mayan calendar.

It was during this second spell at Harvard that Burroughs read *The Wild Party* by Joseph Moncure March, a hard-boiled epic poem about a grimly orgiastic drunken party involving some low theatrical types. Written in 1928, it probably owed something to the *Hollywood Babylon*-style atmosphere of corruption that clung to acting in the wake of the Fatty Arbuckle case. An evil woman seduces a decent man, which leads to him shooting her brutish boyfriend, and at the end the police burst in.

It was controversial in its day, and banned in Boston. The *Times Literary Supplement* described it as 'extremely clever' but said 'a picture of life in which sexual squalor is neither relieved nor measured by any element of human fineness is artistically valueless'.[6] Four or five decades later the graphic artist Art Spiegelman mentioned it to Burroughs and was surprised by the enthusiasm of his recollection: eyes becoming unfocused in the effort of memory, Burroughs suddenly began to recite in a twanging voice:

Queenie was a blonde, and her age stood still
And she danced twice a day in vaudeville . . .

On and on he went, reciting long chunks until the catastrophic end when

The door swung open
And the cops rushed in.

'It's the book that made me want to be a writer',[7] he said.

Burroughs and Kells Elvins collaborated together on a piece of writing entitled 'Twilight's Last Gleamings,' a sick comic sketch

about a *Titanic*-style sinking of a ship called the ss *America* in which
the captain rushes for the lifeboat in drag. 'Twilight's Last Gleamings'
is an all-American debacle, with a sense of nemesis and payback for
the American bourgeoisie: passengers include Philip Bradshinkel,
investment banker, and Branch Morton, St Louis politician, and
while the ship is sinking after an explosion their wives are whisked
away by two members of the 'Negro orchestra', 'high on marihuana',
'their eyes gleaming, saying "Can us have dis dance witchu?"'

The radio operator is tapping out an sos and as he complains
'Goddamed captain's a brown artist' (i.e. a homosexual) the captain comes up behind him in a kimono and wig and blasts him in
the head with a revolver. Meanwhile a wheelchair-bound 'paretic' –
a sufferer from syphilitic paralysis, which Elvins's father suffered
from – is abusing all and sundry with his distinctive paretic impedi-
ment ('you pithy-athed thon of a bidth') and later starts chopping
clambering hands and gripping fingers away from the lifeboat with
a butcher's knife. The jukebox plays the 'Star-Spangled Banner',
ironically intercut with the action, and a female survivor ends up
with a severed finger as a souvenir. 'I don't know', she says, 'I feel
sorta bad about this old finger'.[8]

Like a crazed piece of drama therapy, Burroughs and Elvins
acted out the characters on the ship as they invented the dialogue,
and Burroughs had 'laughing jags. I hadn't laughed like that since
my first tea [cannabis] high at eighteen when I rolled around the
floor and pissed all over myself.'[9]

Burroughs and Elvins sent it to *Esquire*, only to get a rejection
slip: 'Too screwy, and not effectively so for us.' Burroughs was
discouraged, but it still felt like lifting a curse that had been on his
writing ever since the diary at Los Alamos: 'I see now that the curse
of the diary was broken temporarily by the act of collaboration',
he wrote years later.[10]

The Harvard house-share came to an end when Elvins got a job
as a prison psychologist in Huntsville, Texas, and Burroughs visited

him there before moving on to New York. He had meanwhile read a book that greatly impressed him, Alfred Korzybski's *Science and Sanity* (1933), a critique of ordinary and misleading assumptions about language and its relation to reality: it was Korzybski who said 'The map is not the territory.' Count Alfred Korzybski was a former Tsarist intelligence officer who had settled in America after the 1917 revolution, and Burroughs was sufficiently interested in his ideas to go to Chicago in August 1939 to see him give a series of lectures.

> Korzybski points to a chair and says, 'Whatever that may be, it is not a "chair".' That is, it is not the verbal label 'chair'. The *is* of identity which equates the word with the object or process to which the word refers is a source of confusion ranging from muddled thinking and purely verbal arguments to outright insanity. A follower of Korzybski has proposed to delete the verb *to be* from the English language.[11]

Languages like Chinese or ancient Egyptian make less use of this '*is* of identity which, as Alfred Korzybski said, is one of the big fuck-ups of Western language. Something "is" something, with the implication that there is some sort of eternal status conveyed.'[12] Korzybski's position is a form of nominalism, rejecting the reifying effect of nouns: words like 'fascist', 'communist', 'humanist' and 'moralist' were meaningless, and Burroughs tried to avoid them. When Ginsberg asked him what 'art' was, Burroughs said 'A three-letter word.'[13] Another great trap of Western thinking, and in this Korzybski seems to anticipate deconstruction, was the 'either/or' of Aristotelian logic, such that something must either be one thing or another thing. Is the music of the Rolling Stones broadcasting an establishment or anti-establishment message? 'Well, they might be doing both at the same time quite well. Or all sorts of variations. Really it's not an either/or proposition.'[14]

Korzybski was a lifelong influence on Burroughs's thinking, and the explications above are all his own, from the 1970s and '80s. Korzybski has remained a maverick thinker and he has probably had more influence on science-fiction writers – including Frank Herbert, Robert Heinlein, L. Ron Hubbard and A. E. Van Vogt – than he has on professional philosophers.

Back in New York, in 1940, Burroughs developed an unrequited passion for a handsome young man called Jack Anderson. Burroughs managed to get him into bed in a cheap hotel when the house detective suddenly burst in on them, and they were thrown out. Anderson is described in most accounts with words such as hustler and vacuous, and it was not a happy relationship. Whenever Burroughs tried to talk about anything intellectual or serious Anderson would put him down and mock him, saying 'Is that what Count Korzybski says?'[15]

Around this time Burroughs entered into his first full psycho-analysis with a New York Freudian, Dr Herbert Wiggers. Years later he looked back on psychoanalysis as a complete waste of time and money, with the superego and so forth as purely mythological or 'mystical'[16] constructs, but closer to the time he wrote, in *Junky*, that it 'removed inhibitions and anxiety so that I could live the way I wanted to live'.[17] In his most generous later verdict he writes 'Well, something happened and some little key was turned . . . perhaps so that I went on to do what I have done.'[18]

One of Burroughs's central problems, which he probably talked about in analysis, was that he hated effeminacy but at the same time he felt it lurking within him. He was 'queer' but emphatically not a 'faggot', and this influenced his model of the mind, with the *other inside*: the inner fag was the enemy within (a role that he would eventually expand to include language as a virus). This is at least one origin of his decentred, schizoid, almost mediumistic sense of self (or selves) and it also played a major part in his sense of humour. As for fags in the outer world, they seemed *possessed* by an alien force:

'they jerk around like puppets on invisible strings . . . The live human being has moved out of these bodies long ago. But something moved in when the original tenant moved out. Fags are ventriloquists' dummies who have moved in and taken over the ventriloquist.'[19]

Burroughs was being driven to distraction by unhappiness and jealousy over Jack Anderson. Perhaps thinking it would impress him ('a Van Gogh kick . . . to impress someone who interested me', as 'William Lee' casually refers to it in *Junky*[20]) and perhaps as what some people might call a cry for help, Burroughs bought some poultry shears and cut off the last joint of his little finger. As he re-told the incident in a short story, 'The Finger', 'He looked in the mirror, composing his face into the supercilious mask of an eighteenth-century dandy.'

> A moment later, with no physical pain, the finger was off and there was a jab of regret.
>
> He felt a sudden deep pity for the finger joint that lay there on the dresser, a few drops of blood gathering around the white bone. Tears came to his eyes.
>
> 'It didn't do anything,' he said in a broken child's voice.[21]

When Burroughs wrote 'The Finger' he changed the sexes: 'I love her and she's so stupid I can't make an impression. Night after night I lay there hearing her carry on with some man in the next room. It's tearing me all apart . . . So I hit on this finger joint gimmick. I'll present it to her: "A trifling memento of my undying affection. I suggest you wear it around your neck in a pendant filled with formaldehyde."'[22]

A few years later, in one of Burroughs's magnificently crazed hyperboles, he is desperately trying to impress a young man and offers to cut his own foot off, then shrink it down by the shrunken-head process to make the boy a watch fob. All the boy says is 'What I want with your ugly old foot?'[23]

For now Burroughs took the finger not to Jack Anderson but to his analyst Dr Wiggers, who thought he was having a psychotic episode and needed to be hospitalized. Wiggers took him to New York's Bellevue Hospital – for physical first aid, Burroughs thought – only to get him checked him into the psychiatric department and leave him there: 'my analyst, the lousy bastard, shanghaied me into a nuthouse'.[24]

When Burroughs contacted his parents his father came to New York and had him transferred to a private psychiatric hospital, the Payne-Whitney. Here he was given hypno-analysis and narco-analysis, a form of therapy that relies on barbiturates or 'truth drugs' such as sodium pentothal to lower the patient's defences and release repressed material (it has also been used in police interrogation, where it is largely discredited). Burroughs went into almost mediumistic spiels or routines at the Payne-Whitney, with various inner characters and subsidiary personalities coming out: 'During hypno- and narco-analysis, he had these episodes he called "routines" in which he would become a Chinese peasant on the Yangtze, or a redneck farmer in Texas, or a Hungarian dowager duchess.'[25]

Released from the Payne-Whitney, Burroughs went back to his parents' house in St Louis, and worked as a delivery boy for their shop. It was a low ebb, and it was during this period, while he was giving Jack Anderson a driving lesson one night in his father's car, that they crashed near Union Station. America's entry into the War was now foreseeable, and Burroughs tried to enlist, no doubt partly to escape from St Louis.

Thin and short-sighted, Burroughs was rejected at his Navy medical. He then tried the American Field Service, which had been founded by a Harvard professor as a volunteer ambulance-driving service during the First War. Earlier members had included Francophile American writers such as Harry Crosby and Malcolm Cowley. The AFS was socially exclusive, with its members expected to be a credit to America abroad, and Burroughs seems not to have made a good enough impression at his interview.

Along with parachutes, gliders were used as a method of delivering combat troops behind enemy lines, and Burroughs hoped to become a glider pilot. He qualified privately for an aviation licence, clocking up a hundred hours in small planes, but he was still rejected by the Glider Corps because of his bad eyesight. It proved to be exceptionally dangerous work, with a poor life expectancy, and with hindsight this rejection may have been a lucky escape for twentieth-century writing.

The legendary Colonel 'Wild Bill' Donovan was meanwhile setting up a modern security service for America. This would soon become the oss (Office of Strategic Security), the forerunner of the cia. This was something that Burroughs could see himself doing ('I would have been into that whole espionage thing'[26]), and he had a letter of introduction from his uncle Wideman Lee. The two Bills faced each other across the table – an odd moment in American history – and they seem to have got along well enough until Wild Bill introduced his colleague; it was James Phinney Baxter, Burroughs's old Harvard housemaster from the days when he kept a ferret and a gun in his room.

With his attempts to volunteer now rejected all round, Burroughs was back in St Louis. In a last attempt to find him work in New York, his father contacted a friend who ran a small advertising agency, and at last Burroughs was in. As a junior copywriter he handled the unglamorous jobs, like 'Cascade' colonic irrigation, where he excelled himself: 'Well done thou true and faithful servant,' he wrote, 'this is how many people feel about their Cascade . . . You feel as if reborn.'[27]

Burroughs was now sharing an apartment with Jack Anderson and making the best of the relatively stable situation, although on one occasion it led him into a fight with Anderson's jealous girlfriend. Then the Japanese bombed Pearl Harbor, and the situation changed. Burroughs was drafted into the infantry at Jefferson Barracks near St Louis.

Becoming an infantry private was not what Burroughs or his parents had in mind, and his mother pulled some strings and drew attention to her son's psychiatric record. Burroughs was now in limbo, waiting to leave the army, and in the evenings his devoted parents would drive out to the barracks taking him food. It was at this period, in barracks, that Burroughs read the whole of Proust's *A la Recherche de temps perdu*, 'in search of lost time'.

Burroughs later felt himself close to Proust as a writer – closer than he was to Beckett, specifically – particularly in their creation of memorable, larger than life characters like Charlus and Benway and Swann and Kim Carsons. There was Proust's insight into love as generally unreciprocal, an 'algebra of desire'[28] caused by our association of the beloved's image with the things we don't have or are excluded from, and Proust's whole comic take on European high society, and 'the poetry in snobbery'.[29] Above all there was the central Proustian miracle of sudden, vivid subjective time-travel by means of association: the feel of an uneven paving stone, the taste of a madeleine cake dipped in tea. 'Like Proust I am very much concerned with Time and Memory; with tracing the lines of association and the intersection of points of memory'; 'in Proust, time is everything. The memory traces evocations of memory on lines of association. It's all Pavlov.'[30] Jerk the handle, and the result is the same for given co-ordinates.

While he was at Jefferson Barracks Burroughs met an Irishman from Chicago, Ray Masterson, who told him there were plenty of jobs there in the Windy City. Once he got out of the army in September 1942 Burroughs went to Chicago, at first plunging into blue-collar life with a short-lived factory job and moving on to slightly seedier and more equivocal jobs such as being a private detective – he worked for a short time with Merrit Inc., who specialized in catching employees with their hands in the till – and most famously as an exterminator, remembered in his book of the same name.

The swingeing, no-nonsense harshness of the word suits Burroughs's later image, like his persona on the job itself, 'in his forties trilby hat and trenchcoat', as Barry Miles has written, '. . . like something out of Raymond Chandler'.[31] Burroughs worked for A. J. Cohen Ltd, remembered with flat but atmospheric precision; 'ground floor office dead-end street by the river.'[32] He used his own car, a black Ford v-8, travelling with his bedbug spray, pyrethrum powder, bellows and fluoride, and he understood the work; chatting with the customers, dealing with the roaches, bending the Board of Health regulations where required, and accepting back-handers and cups of tea.

> I liked the cafeteria basement jobs long grey basement you can't see the end of it white dust drifting as I trace arabesques of fluoride on the wall.
> We serviced an old theatrical hotel rooms with rose wallpaper photograph albums . . . 'Yes that's me there on the left.'

Like the British rag and bone men, or the itinerant glaziers who used to walk the streets of Paris with sheet glass on their backs shouting 'Viiiiitrier . . .!' Burroughs depicts himself hawking for trade, shouting out and knocking from door to door.

> From a great distance I see a cool remote naborhood blue windy day in April sun cold on your exterminator there climbing the grey wooden outside stairs.
> 'Exterminator lady. You need the service?'

At eight or nine months it was his record in work until eventually he left, shaking hands with all the Cohen brothers.

> A distant cry echoes down cobblestone streets through all the grey basements up the outside stairs to a windy blue sky.
> 'Exterminator!'

3

New York, New York

Burroughs had two friends from St Louis in Chicago, Lucien Carr and David Kammerer. They were an odd pair; Carr was seventeen, largely heterosexual and strikingly good-looking, while Kammerer was 31 – around three years older than Burroughs – queer, and obsessed by Carr. They are sometimes said to have met when Kammerer was Carr's scoutmaster, and if not the Scouts it was a youth group of some kind that Kammerer supervised. Carr was literary, pretentious and deviant, reading Rimbaud and drinking Pernod as the nearest thing to absinthe. While he was in Chicago he tried to gas himself, and afterwards told the psychiatrist it was a work of art.

When Carr went to New York in 1943, to attend Columbia University, Kammerer followed, and Burroughs followed the pair of them. It was through Carr that the nucleus of the so-called Beat Generation – Jack Kerouac, Allen Ginsberg and Burroughs – came together. Ginsberg, also studying at Columbia, was a literary, spiritual and slightly disturbed young man, troubled by his sexuality and his schizophrenic mother. He was fascinated by Carr's mind and angelic looks and wrote about him in his journal, recording his idiosyncratic language and listing his 'fetishes', which included Mahler, Pernod, 'Burroughs at 48 Morton' and knives.[1]

Burroughs was living at 69 Bedford Street, and the address at 48 Morton Street, where Carr would see him, was Kammerer's place around the corner. One day Carr took Ginsberg along, and

Ginsberg was impressed by Burroughs's casual quotation of Shakespeare, unusual knowledge and idiosyncratic take on things. Meanwhile Jack Kerouac, a high-school football star and former merchant seaman, was also at Columbia, and when Burroughs said he wanted to join the merchant marine Carr introduced him to Kerouac for advice.

Kerouac was married to Edie Parker, who shared an apartment with a Columbia journalism student named Joan Vollmer. From around Christmas 1943 and into 1944, the group of them – Carr, Ginsberg, Kerouac and Burroughs, but not Kammerer, and three women: Edie, Joan, and another girl named Celine Young – formed what Ginsberg called 'the libertine circle'. Meeting Ginsberg ('this spindly Jewish kid with horn-rimmed glasses and tremendous ears sticking out . . . burning black eyes, a strangely deep mature voice') Kerouac had been struck by something lecherous about him, as if he wanted 'everybody in the world to take a bath in the same huge bathtub which would give him a chance to feel legs under the dirty water'.[2]

At almost thirty Burroughs was around ten years older than the others, and he was the wise man of the group. He knew how to eat with chopsticks, and he would quote Alexander Pope and lend them books such as Jean Cocteau's *Opium* and Spengler's *Decline of the West*. Handing the full two volumes of Spengler to Kerouac, he might say 'Edify your mind, my boy, with the grand actuality of fact.'[3] And then there was the enduring influence of Korzybski: 'Watch your semantics, young man', he could say to Ginsberg, or 'Human, Allen, is an adjective and its use as a noun is in itself regrettable.'[4]

Carr and Kammerer were given to wild behaviour. Once they were at the Morton Street apartment when Carr bit his glass and started chewing up the pieces. Not to be outdone, Kammerer started crunching his. Like the perfect host, Burroughs went into the kitchen and emerged a moment later with a plate of razor blades and lightbulbs, saying his mother had sent him some delicacies.[5]

One night Kammerer climbed the fire escape to Carr's dormitory at Columbia, got himself through a window, and stood there watching Carr sleep. Carr was oppressed by Kammerer's attentions; he went to join the merchant marine with Kerouac to get away from him, but they failed to get their ship.

Early in the morning of 14 August 1944, there was a knock on Burroughs's door. Burroughs opened it in his dressing gown to find Carr standing there in an agitated state. 'I just killed the old man', he said, and offered Burroughs the last cigarette from a blood-stained packet of Lucky Strikes. Kammerer and Carr had been drinking by the Hudson river, between three and four in the morning, when Kammerer had become wild, pawing Carr about and threatening to harm his girlfriend. A struggle ensued and Carr stabbed him through the heart with his Boy Scout knife, dumping the body in the river.

Now he was facing the electric chair, but Burroughs (pacing up and down and putting on 'his best Claude Rains manner'[6]) thought he could get off if he played his cards right. He advised him to give himself up and plead self-defence. Burroughs disposed of the bloody cigarette packet in small pieces down the lavatory and Carr went on to see Kerouac. They disposed of the knife down a drain and went to the Museum of Modern Art and the movies, where they saw the 1939 film of A.E.W. Mason's *The Four Feathers*, with British soldiers and rebels slaughtering each other in Egypt. Trying to forget the day's events, they winced to find a character in the film called Burroughs.

Carr duly gave himself up, and Kerouac and Burroughs were arrested for failing to report a homicide. Burroughs's father arrived and posted $2,500 bail. The Carr case ('Student is Silent on Slaying Friend') shared the papers with the war in Europe, where General Patton's Third Army was driving south from Normandy. Journalists were struck by Carr's studious manner and lack of emotion, and by the 'poetry-reading killer' angle. He appeared in court holding a book – Yeats's *A Vision*, in fact not poetry but mediumistic spirit writing – which he had borrowed from Burroughs.

The case hinged on whether Carr was queer or not, as Burroughs thought it would. It was either a sordid fight between two homosexuals, in which case Carr was in deep trouble, or it was an upstanding young man defending himself against the advances of a pederast. Burroughs and Kerouac were repeatedly asked about Carr's sexual orientation. As for Kammerer, a man from the Homicide Bureau asked Burroughs if he knew Kammerer was a homosexual. 'Yes,' said Burroughs, 'I frequently remonstrated with him but in vain.'[7]

Carr got off lightly, serving two years. Kerouac and Burroughs collaborated together on a novel about the case, originally entitled 'I Wish I Was You'. They retitled it 'And The Hippos Were Boiled In Their Tanks', seemingly after a snatch of radio news about a fire at a circus. Burroughs also associated this kind of surrealistic news with the experiments of a friend called Jerry Newman, who made a scrambled tape called 'The Drunken Newscaster'.[8]

Burroughs and Kerouac wrote as 'Seward Lewis' (their middle names) with alternate chapters narrated by 'Will Dennison' and 'Mike Ryko': Burroughs wrote Dennison and Kerouac Ryko. The first chapter, by Dennison, introduces seventeen-year-old Phillip Tourian, 'the kind of boy literary fags write sonnets to', and Ramsay Allen, 'hovering over him like a shy vulture'. 'Al is one of the best guys I know and you couldn't find better company. And Phillip is all right too.' But when they got together, Burroughs wrote, they formed a combination that got on everyone's nerves: pissing out of windows, eating glass and generally horsing around with 'Joe College stuff about 1910 style'.[9]

They failed to get it published, adding to Burroughs's discouragement with writing. Kerouac would be published first, becoming famous while Burroughs was still obscure, but he always urged Burroughs not to give up on his writerly destiny: 'You can't walk out on the Shakespeare Squadron, Bill.'[10]

Meanwhile Burroughs's interest in psychoanalysis continued. In Chicago he had been analysed by Kurt Eissler, and in New York he had analysis with the eminent Dr Paul Federn, a former Viennese colleague of Freud. Federn described Burroughs as a 'Gangsterling' – a wannabe criminal[11] – while Burroughs remembered him as a 'nice old gentleman' and found him a generally sympathetic figure, but they disagreed when Burroughs tried to talk about the reality of telepathic influence and witchcraft: witches were just hysterics, said Federn, and their victims were paranoids.[12]

Burroughs considered training as an analyst himself, and he was giving lay or 'wild' psychoanalysis to Kerouac and Ginsberg, getting them to free associate, which Ginsberg found painful. Ginsberg wrote to Wilhelm Reich, asking Reich to recommend an analyst to help him with his 'psychic difficulties' in being homosexual, and described his amateur analysis with Burroughs as having left him 'with a number of my defenses broken, but, centrally unchanged, with nothing to replace the lost armor'.[13]

One of the larger ideas Burroughs must have encountered in psychoanalysis is the whole area of identification and introjection, in which other people – parents, for example – are taken inside the psyche like colonists or parasites and then control it from within. The Freudian super-ego was said to have been formed by introjected parents or parental values, like the 1960s idea of the inner policeman or sleeping cop inside. In Proust, the lesbian Mlle Vinteuil glories in the fact that her father is dead, but she still seems to be turning into him with her phrases and mannerisms; she can't escape so easily. It was a popular mid-twentieth century explanation of male homosexuality to say that the man had identified with – or introjected, or internalized – his mother (or grandmother, or big sister, or whoever). When Burroughs invented his satirical categories of evil people who impinge on others, such as 'Liquefactionists', 'Senders' and 'Divisionists', the 'Senders' were figures who over-influenced their victims to the extent that they took their identities over, reproducing themselves in others by a kind of imprinting. 'Queers have been worked over by female Senders. They are a reminder of what the Senders can and will do unless they are stopped.'[14]

It is like the 'foul and unnatural act whereby a boy's mother take over his body and infiltrate [*sic*] her horrible old substance' in *The Soft Machine*,[15] or as Burroughs cautions readers a couple of decades later in *The Western Lands*, 'Remember that the Egyptian glyph for poltroon is woman as man, that is, a female Ka [soul or spirit self] taking over a male body.'[16]

Sexuality may have been central to the origin of Burroughs' decentred and schizoid self, but the implications of his ideas of identification and possession go much further, along with his significance as a writer. Psychoanalysis itself, for example, is suspect because of the way analysts imprint themselves on their patients. Referring to Ginsberg's 'normality programme', he wrote to Kerouac that his therapists had 'reconstructed him in their own dreary image'[17]).

Burroughs found that the boundaries of his own self were more generally adrift when his interest in Egyptian hieroglyphics took him to the Egyptology department of the University of Chicago in 1939, and a voice was screaming at him 'YOU DON'T BELONG HERE!'

> This occasion was my first clear indication of something in my being that was not me, and not under my control. I remember a dream from this period . . . In the dream I am floating up near the ceiling with a feeling of utter death and despair, and looking down I see my body walking out the door with deadly purpose.[18]

Federn referred Burroughs to Dr Lewis Wolberg, with whom he stayed in analysis until late 1946. Wolberg's speciality was hypnoanalysis, and he published an influential book of that title in 1945. Combining psychoanalysis with hypnosis, hypnoanalysis seemed to be at the cutting edge of American psychotherapy. Another book on it, Robert Lindner's 1944 *Rebel Without A Cause: The Hypnoanalysis of a Criminal Psychopath*, became the inspiration for the James Dean film.

Like his time in the Payne-Whitney, hypnoanalysis seemed to reveal subsidiary personalities at various levels of Burroughs's psyche, including a Southern bigot of a sheriff and 'a simpering English governess, always shrieking and giggling'.[19] In the same vein, Burroughs, Ginsberg, Kerouac and another friend called Hal Chase would act out comic routines together (like Burroughs and Elvins back at Harvard). Ginsberg would pretend to be a smooth and crooked *Mitteleuropean* who wanted to sell phoney heirlooms to a couple of naive Americans in the shape of Chase and Kerouac. Ginsberg's accomplice in this was a woman played by Burroughs in drag, 'an Edith Sitwell character, vaguely lesbian'.[20] A relative of hers would come out again in the early 1960s, when Burroughs wrote as Lady Sutton-Smith. As Barry Miles has noted, these comic routines were absolutely central to Burroughs's development as a writer, pushing fantastic situations to a surreal breaking point. They also had an element of mediumistic impersonation and giving vent to inner 'voices', and in that sense they were not so distant from something Burroughs might catch himself doing in ordinary speech: 'My Gawd,' he might suddenly say, 'I sound just like a dreary old Ka-*Ween*!'[21]

These acting sessions took place in the large 115th Street apartment originally shared by Joan Vollmer, Edie Parker and Kerouac, with Chase, Ginsberg and Burroughs moving in later. Burroughs got on well with Joan, and Ginsberg and Kerouac wanted to put them together: 'Jack and I decided that Joan and Bill would make a great couple', Ginsberg remembered, 'They were a match for each other . . . equally tuned and equally witty and funny and intelligent and equally well read, equally refined.'[22]

Joan Vollmer in the Forties, photographed by Allen Ginsberg.

Around ten years younger than Bill, Joan was an elegant young woman and a great reader: she could talk about philosophy, and she liked to read Proust, or simply the newspapers, in a bubble bath. She had been married and had a young daughter, Julie, and she was a strong character and sexually outspoken. She told Burroughs he made love like a pimp (intended as a compliment, and one that Burroughs always took pride in). They become lovers in 1945, and at least initially they were great companions for each other. She was interested in the Mayans and talked about their control powers, suggesting to Burroughs that they may have had telepathic control over the people.

In due course she came to regard herself as Burroughs's common-law wife, and he liked to be able to refer to her casually as his 'old lady', like an ordinary man in a bar. At one point they clocked up an arrest for public indecency when the police caught them having sex on the roadside beside their parked vehicle. Burroughs was bailed out by his parents after a night in jail and fined $173.

Burroughs had long been fascinated by crime and the underworld, and he had already planned, or fantasized, schemes to stick up a Turkish bath for the takings and knock over an armoured Brink's Mat lorry, catching it with a bomb as it went over a manhole. Early in 1946, seemingly through Jack Anderson, an acquaintance named Norman ('Norton' in *Junky*) approached Burroughs with a stolen submachine gun he wanted to sell. Burroughs was interested, and Norman produced something else he wanted to get rid of; he had some syrettes of morphine.

Burroughs was a regular customer at the soda fountain in a drugstore near Columbia University, and he had come to know the soda jerk there, a petty criminal with a gangsterish personal style named Bob Brandenburg ('Jack' in *Junky*). After talking about the gun, Brandenburg took Burroughs to meet his flatmates, a hustler named Herbert Huncke ('Herman' in *Junky*) and another petty criminal and psychopath named Phil White, also known as The Sailor ('Roy' in *Junky*). Phil the Sailor had a Southern accent, an oddly asymmetrical skull and peculiarly bright eyes, which Burroughs remembered glinting like opals.

Huncke, also known as Huncke the Junky, was a well-known figure around Times Square. He was a small man with heavy-lidded eyes and a faintly exotic or Eastern appearance. He had spent years in and out of imprisonment and existed as a prostitute and low thief, but he was also noted as a raconteur and later wrote books, ending his days in a small room in the Chelsea Hotel paid for by the Grateful Dead.

He wasn't very taken by Burroughs when he first turned up at the apartment. Burroughs seemed extremely square and dull. His spectacles, snap-brim hat and out-of-fashion Chesterfield coat gave him a distinctly conservative appearance, and it occurred to Huncke that he was a plain clothes policeman, perhaps even an FBI man. Huncke wanted Burroughs to leave, but he seemed to be hitting it off with Phil White, especially after he mentioned the morphine.

Still wary, Huncke declined to buy any, but White was keen. Burroughs kept a couple of syrettes for himself, and – as Huncke remembered it – said rather earnestly 'The one or two I keep I'd like to try taking – in order to see what the experience of taking an addictive drug is like. Have either of you any knowledge of this stuff, and if so do you know how it is taken?'[23]

This made The Sailor laugh. Unknown to Burroughs they were both junkies, and they had just come back from a long sea voyage taken with the intent of quitting. Instead, like something out of 'Twilight's Last Gleamings', they had met a bent orderly who kept them in morphine by rifling the ship's medical supplies, and they came back with their habits as bad as ever.

It was the start of Burroughs's long involvement with opiates, which have had a special relationship to mankind since Cro-Magnon times.[24] There is a concept in Buddhism called *dukkha*, sometimes translated as suffering, but with a wider sense of nagging discomfort, frustration, sadness and the whole underlying dissatisfaction that attends being, and particularly being-in-time. Opiates are the anti-*dukkha* drug, the drug that makes everything all right. Or as British writer Edward St Aubyn puts it, 'Heroin was the missing chair leg, made with such precision that it matched every splinter of the break.'[25]

'It has been compared', John Jones wrote in his 1700 book *Mysteries of Opium Reveal'd*, 'to a permanent gentle degree of that pleasure which modesty forbids the name of',[26] and Burroughs writes of users as 'customers of fossil orgasm'.[27] As well as an upwelling of pleasure, the sense of warmth, plenitude and collectedness is completely distinct from the excitable stupefactions of drinking, as De Quincey writes:

> Wine robs a man of his self-possession: opium greatly invigorates it . . . communicates serenity and equipoise to all the faculties, active or passive . . . [it] always seems to compose what had been agitated, and to concentrate what had been distracted. In short . . . [alcohol] calls up into supremacy the merely human, too often the brutal . . . but the opium-eater . . . feels that the diviner part of his nature is paramount.[28]

At the same time opiates can bring a sensation of something abyssal, or a doominess at the edges: Burroughs had a feeling that 'some horrible image was just beyond the field of vision, moving, as I turned my head, so that I never quite saw it.'[29] But this is not the real horror of excessive opiate use, which is notoriously that the early pleasures drop away and cannot be recaptured, and the addict needs the drug just to feel normal instead of unbearable.

For now, Burroughs felt 'a spreading wave of relaxation' so he seemed 'to float without outlines, like lying in warm salt water'.[30] He soon learned to enjoy it, settling into a grey cocoon of safety and comfort. As Huncke says, 'It was the beginning of a whole new life for Bill.'[31]

A few years later, from the perspective of addiction, Burroughs could say simply 'Junk is not a kick. It is a way of life.'[32] More than that, for Burroughs it became a way of *seeing* life. Addiction – to love, to language, to control – became central to his reading of the world, the obverse of his concern with freedom and escape.

Burroughs's new life also meant hanging out with Phil 'the Sailor' White, and gradually Huncke became reconciled to him.

From that first meeting, when Burroughs felt 'waves of hostility and suspicion' flowing from his eyes 'like some sort of television broadcast',[33] Huncke came to think 'just possibly he was a nice person trying to experience something a bit more exciting than what he was usually involved with . . .'.[34] Before long Huncke was mooching small sums of cash from Burroughs and letting him buy drinks and meals.

Huncke and White were Burroughs's entry to a criminal circle. There was a Little Jack Melody and his girlfriend Vickie Russell (aka Priscilla Armitage, 'Mary' in *Junky*). The daughter of a judge, Vickie Russell was a head taller than Little Jack and besotted with him: 'I'm queer for Jack.'[35] Then there was Bill Garver ('Bill Gains' in *Junky*), whom Huncke had met in prison. Garver was a middle-aged, middle-class junky from a good family who kept his credentials and general 'claims to reality' in an old manila envelope, including a card to the Masons, and supported himself by the specialized crime of stealing overcoats from restaurants and pawning them. For Burroughs, Gains was so invisibly respectable he was like a ghost:

> There is a certain kind of ghost that can only materialize with the aid of a sheet or other piece of cloth to give it outline. Gains was like that. He materialized in someone else's overcoat.[36]

Garver was a typical junky in being middle-aged: junkies were older then, often 'beat' old guys working as waiters or janitors ('spectral janitors, grey as ashes, phantom porters sweeping out dusty halls with a slow old man's hand, coughing and spitting in the junk-sick dawn, retired asthmatic fences in theatrical hotels . . .'.[37])

It was a Jack Black world that Burroughs found himself in: 'old time thieves, pickpockets and people like that. They're a dying race; very few of those old timers left . . . they were show business.'[38] Burroughs was fascinated by the mysteries of short-change artists:

> They had something called The Bill, a short-change deal. I've never been able to figure out how it works. One man I knew beat all the cashiers in Grand Central with this thing. It starts with a $20 bill. You give them a $20 bill and then when you get the change you say, 'Well, wait a minute, I must have been dreaming. I've got the change after all.' First thing you know, the cashier's short $10 . . . When they got in court and tried to explain what had happened, none of them could do it. I keep stories like this in my files.[39]

One of the landmarks in Burroughs's new world, recorded in *Junky*, was the Angle Bar at the corner of 8th Avenue and 42nd Street. The proto-Beat crew went there for a while, rubbing shoulders with small-time criminals. Huncke would tell stories there about people he had known, and he also recruited subjects for Dr Kinsey's sex researches, including Burroughs, who was interviewed by Kinsey's assistant Wardle Pomeroy. Recalling 'a year of low, evil decadence' and 'furtive evil characters', Kerouac remembered 'We hung out in the evil bar on 8th Avenue around the corner from 42nd Street.'[40]

Writing to Ginsberg later, Burroughs described *Junky* as a travel book.[41] In one sense it is a travel book through the hell of the underworld, an 'anthropo-sociological travelogue' as Alan Ansen has called it,[42] but Burroughs's comment in the letter to Ginsberg is focused on junk itself as the object of this 'travel' account. *Junky* is the start of Burroughs's writing as a journey through psychic spaces and drugscapes, where even junk – not usually considered a 'trippy' drug – showed him a distinctive cityscape:

> A series of pictures passed, like watching a movie: A huge, neon-lighted cocktail bar that got larger and larger until streets,

traffic, and street repairs were included in it; a waitress carrying a skull on a tray; stars in the clear sky.[43]

More than just providing an all-purpose metaphorical schema of need, the quality of opiates would from now on infuse Burroughs's writing and his very personal landscapes:

> I lay there looking at shadows on the white plaster ceiling. I remembered a long time ago when I lay in bed beside my mother, watching lights from the street move across the ceiling and down the walls. I felt the sharp nostalgia of train whistles, piano music down a city street, burning leaves.
>   A mild degree of junk sickness always brought me the magic of childhood. 'It never fails,' I thought. 'Just like a shot. I wonder if all junkies score for this wonderful stuff.'[44]

As Ann Marlowe writes in *How To Stop Time: An A–Z of Heroin*, 'Heroin addiction is essentially nostalgic.'[45] Although her primary meaning seems to be recapturing the first experience of the drug, it is a statement with a larger resonance: Eric Detzer, in *Monkey on My Back*, writes 'Even the first time, the experience is old and familiar, like reliving your seventh birthday.'[46]

Burroughs went further into the underworld and into heroin than his Beat friends. Ginsberg was an occasional recreational user of heroin, while Kerouac tried it and didn't like it. Kerouac's drug of choice was amphetamines, a weakness he shared with Burroughs's common-law wife Joan. These were popular in the form of Benzedrine inhalers, which could be bought over the counter and cracked open to remove the Benzedrine. Burroughs tried Benzedrine inhalers with Vickie Russell in a late-night eatery. After washing the Benzedrine down with coffee, he found himself talking rapidly and suddenly full of 'expansive, benevolent feelings', wanting to call on people he hadn't seen in years, 'people I did not like and who did not like me'. Vickie meanwhile selected some real 'gone numbers' on the jukebox, and started to beat on the table 'with the expression of a masturbating idiot'.[47]

Kerouac and Joan both suffered from their Benzedrine abuse. Kerouac developed phlebitis in his legs, while Joan saw tiny worms on her skin, became delusional and heard non-existent arguments in the flat downstairs. Burroughs had meanwhile developed a hard drug habit, and in April 1946 he was arrested over a forged prescription for Dilaudid, from a stolen prescription pad. The two detectives who came for him – like Hauser and O'Brien in *Naked Lunch* – played the soft cop / hard cop routine, 'the con man and tough guy team'.[48]

Burroughs was briefly imprisoned in the Tombs, a New York prison, before Dr Wolberg informed his parents and his father came to bail him out. Far from going straight before his case came up, Burroughs dealt heroin in Greenwich Village with Bill Garver and tried 'lush working' – robbing sleeping drunks on the metro, or 'the Hole', with Phil White (as in the opening line of *The Soft Machine*, 'I was working the hole with the Sailor').

Huncke found the idea of an educated man like Burroughs as White's partner in crime ridiculous, and Burroughs was disturbed when a drunk woke up and things turned violent. In fact White was – in the words of a headline – the MAD DOG NOONDAY KILLER. He borrowed a .32 handgun from Burroughs and went to rob a furrier, who started to shout. White shot him dead. He was never caught, and White and Huncke dismantled Burroughs's gun, dropping it all over New York in pieces.

White came to a bad end, informing on a fellow criminal and then hanging himself in the Tombs in 1951. Burroughs liked and admired White and originally intended to dedicate *Junky* to his memory: as he wrote to Ginsberg, he felt White was 'quite a man'.[49]

Burroughs's case came up in June 1946. It was the first offence of an educated young man from a respectable family, and the judge gave him a four-month suspended sentence. 'Young man,' he said, 'I am going to inflict a terrible punishment on you. I am going to send you home to St Louis for the summer.'[50]

4

Go South, Young Man

Returning to St Louis in the summer of 1946, Burroughs was pleased to find Kells Elvins was there with his wife and son, after war service as a US Marine captain. Elvins and Burroughs dreamed up get-rich-quick patents together (of the everlasting lightbulb variety, including a home dry-cleaning machine) but Elvins had a more solid option with farming, and he persuaded Burroughs to join him. Elvins was growing citrus and cotton in Texas, and Burroughs bought fifty acres of cotton land with money from his parents. The two men rented a house in Pharr, Texas, where they had little to do except gaze at their investment; the work was in the hands of Mexican wetback labour. They had some local cronies and drinking time began daily at five, when Kells would bang a tin pan and they would all jump up, 'like fighters coming out at the bell'.[1]

Joan was still in New York, where her life deteriorated, and in October 1946 she landed in the psychiatric ward at Bellevue. Burroughs went to rescue her, collecting her around 31 October and telling her about the new life they could have in Texas. They checked into a cheap hotel in Times Square and it was there, they later felt, that their child was conceived.

Burroughs left his cotton in the capable hands of Elvins while he pursued a new scheme, growing marijuana with a few opium poppies on the side, in a more remote location at New Waverley ('Man, are we ever in Hicksville'). He and Joan lived there with

Joan's little daughter Julie and Herbert Huncke. Huncke ran errands, buying Joan's benzedrine on wholesale terms in Houston, and generally helped around the place, cooking, and winding the gramophone on which Burroughs listened to Coleman Hawkins's 'Low Flame' and the not very cool Viennese waltzes he liked. 'Aw man, you don't want to listen to that', Huncke would say. 'Oh,' Burroughs would say, 'but I do.'[2]

On 21 July 1947 Joan gave birth to a son, William Seward Burroughs III. She was unable to breastfeed because of the Benzedrine in her system, but Billy had already been thoroughly infused with it during pregnancy. The indications are that he was born addicted and went through withdrawal as an unhappy, difficult infant.

It was during his time in Texas that Burroughs started to study Wilhelm Reich, a maverick former Freudian – analysed, like Burroughs, by Paul Federn – who had taken the sexual basis of psychoanalysis far further than Freud with his new pseudo-science of Orgonomy. Orgasms and sexual satisfaction were the key to psychic and physical health, whereas repression and sexual frustration caused fascism and cancer. 'Orgone energy' from orgasms was not only measurable but blue in colour, which is why the sky is blue. Orgone energy was the good force in the universe, but there was also a bad one – Deadly Orgone Radiation, or DOR for short – which could come from atomic power and manifested itself in evil clouds. These could be dispersed with a Reichian 'cloud buster', an apparatus that pointed upwards like an anti-aircraft gun.

One of Reich's more useful ideas was 'character armour'. This saw character as a defensive residue of resistances and repressions, affecting an individual's whole manner and persona. Burroughs later noted that Peruvian boys were the least character-armoured people he had ever seen ('shit or piss anywhere they feel like it . . . have no inhibitions about expressing affection . . . climb all over each other and hold hands . . .') whereas when a naval lieutenant started to lower his inhibitions, goosing a waiter and acting exhibitionistically towards Burroughs, he described the performance as 'a hideous strip tease with his character armor. Everybody yelling "For God's sake keep it on."'[3]

Burroughs was less interested in Reichian theory than its pseudo-practical application: in particular, he built himself a Reichian 'orgone accumulator', a box large enough for a person to get inside made from alternate layers of metallic and organic materials, causing a health-giving concentration of orgone energy. Burroughs wrote to Kerouac that he had built an orgone accumulator, and it really worked: Reich wasn't mad after all, he was 'a fucking genius'.[4] In *On The Road*, Kerouac has his Burroughs character say 'Say, why don't you fellows try my orgone accumulator? Put some juice in your bones. I always rush up and take off ninety miles an hour for the nearest whorehouse . . .'.[5] Burroughs used an orgone box on and off for the rest of his life.

It was also around this period that Burroughs discovered the English writer Denton Welch (1915–1948), whose books manage to be both exquisitely precious and completely unpretentious. Welch remained an invalid after a 1935 accident that shortened his life, when he was hit by a car while cycling, and his gently feverish writing was much admired by Edith Sitwell among others. In later years Burroughs said Welch was the strongest stylistic influence on his own work, and he combined Welch and himself into Kim Carsons, the teenage hero of his last two novels.

J. G. Ballard once described Burroughs as 'one of the least likely people ever to worry about a carrot crop'.[6] Unlikely or not, Burroughs was always about to make a fortune from his farming, but he never did. His letters to Ginsberg are filled with the exciting prospects for cotton, lettuce, peas, carrots, selling citrus fruit by mail-order and even an oil deal.[7] Unfortunately these hopes are all matched by details of frost, gluts, bottoms dropping out of markets, crops ploughed under and labour costs.

Ginsberg was concerned about the low wages Burroughs was paying, but Burroughs reminded him that without profits there would be no wages at all. The wetback labour scene had its ugly side: it was handled by labour brokers, and one broker mentioned casually that his foreman had shot two wetbacks the previous night. Burroughs didn't have anything to do with it personally, he wrote, but he was struck by the fact that his 'ethical position', as a respectable farmer, was shakier than when he was a drug dealer.[8]

For all that, he worried about the 'perverted' socialist views that Ginsberg was 'infected' by. Burroughs felt bogged down by an 'octopus of bureaucratic socialism', with the USA in danger of becoming like England: 'a Socialistic police state'. Socialism and communism were synonymous, he said, and both were 'unmitigated evil'.[9] It is probably this animus towards socialism that underlies the incongruous obscenity of his later comic routine 'Roosevelt After Inauguration', Roosevelt and his New Deal being distinctly left-of-centre by American standards.

What Burroughs really hated, all his life, was interference. He had Border Patrol Agents deporting his workers, and Department of Agriculture bureaucrats telling him what to plant, and he wasn't going to stand for it: let these people try to take over, he said, and they would learn that 'we are not liberals'.[10] At the time Burroughs was writing this, Wilhelm Reich was being hounded by the Food and Drugs Administration over his beloved orgone box, resulting in his imprisonment by the state bureaucracy and his premature death.

For all Burroughs's gun-toting defence of 'us farmers', the only crop that really went well was his miniature sideline in opium, and he was able to send a ball of it as a present to Ginsberg. The larger fiasco of Farmer Bill is well represented by his luck with marijuana. Having harvested the crop, he packed it in mason jars and transported it 1,900 miles to New York (helped by Beat Generation driver Neal Cassady, 'Dean Moriarty' in *On the Road*; Cassady and Ginsberg had been to stay for a few days). Having reached

New York, he found there was no market for the uncured leaf, and eventually he was relieved to get rid of it for $100. He writes ruefully in *Junky* – as worldly-wise in writing as he was unlucky in reality – 'Pushing weed looks good on paper, like fur farming or raising frogs.'[11]

Burroughs had managed to get off junk, but during this stay in New York Bill Garver got him re-addicted. Burroughs was constantly getting off hard drugs – his letters to Ginsberg are full of assurances that he has quit, and couldn't get a habit again even if he wanted to – only to fall back again, and in January 1948 he voluntarily checked himself into the detoxification centre at Lexington, but with only temporary results. As if to justify the paranoid worldview of Burroughs's later years, Lexington was – unknown to Burroughs at the time – being used by the CIA for clandestine LSD experiments on the patients.

By now Burroughs was tired of living in Hicksville, and he decided to keep his farming interests but move to New Orleans. He arrived in the summer of 1948 for what turned out to be a short and vexing stay. After staying in a rooming house at 111 Transcontinental Drive, in August he moved with Joan and the children to 509 Wagner Street, in the suburb of Algiers, where he soon ran into neighbour troubles. One of the next-door children threw a stone that hit little Billy in the head, and in November he reported to Ginsberg that he was feuding with his neighbours, 'a termite nest of Dagos'. He thought it might escalate but he was ready: 'I've got enough guns here to stand off a siege.'[12]

The word beat, used by Burroughs to mean defeated or wretched – a lousy town would be a beat place – was meanwhile acquiring a more positive sense for Kerouac, amounting almost to beatific. Together with a friend called Al Hinckle, Kerouac and Cassady were driving coast to coast for the sheer hell of it. This kind of beat behaviour was completely alien to Burroughs, and he viewed their trip – recorded in *On The Road* – with a cold eye.

Burroughs's cool and knowing stance was always hip rather than beat, and he was about as likely to drive across America for fun as he was to play the bongos.

He had a further reason for disliking this particular trip, which was that Cassady and co. had left Hinckle's new bride Helen ('Galatea Dunkel' in *On The Road*) marooned in New Orleans, where Burroughs had to put her up. Burroughs found her an honourable and helpful guest but he resented Hinckle and Cassady parking her on him. In a January 1949 letter, notably free from his later misogyny, he writes that nobody deserved such treatment, and certainly not 'a decent, honest, well-meaning, well-mannered Jewish girl like Helen'.[13]

Burroughs was persisting with his farming and he had some new interests in real estate (leading to a lawsuit to get sitting tenants out; there were a couple of 'insufferable fruits' already in the property he was hoping to let[14]) but he hadn't been in New Orleans long when he met a junky named Joe Ricks ('Pat' in *Junky*) and now he was solidly back on junk. A policeman had recognized Ricks in a car with Burroughs and stopped them, leading to a search of Burroughs's house, where incriminating correspondence about marijuana was found.

Burroughs was facing two to five years in a particularly ugly prison, Angola, and if he was caught with anything else before his case came up that would count as a second offence, carrying seven years. His only chance was that the police had searched his house without a warrant, so his lawyer advised trying for a *nulle prosse*. Burroughs checked into a sanatorium, where he went through a painful withdrawal. His lawyer, a man named Link ('Tige' in *Junky*, 'Crile' in Morgan) got the case postponed for a while, but he couldn't stave it off indefinitely. When Burroughs mentioned Texas and Mexico, Link told him about a client who had gone to Venezuela and never come back. He seemed to be hinting that Burroughs might like to do the same.

Burroughs was sick of America, which seemed to him like a police state. You couldn't take drugs, you couldn't have sex by the roadside, you couldn't evict tenants from your own property, you couldn't stop the police barging into your house and taking your letters away; it was too much. After another spell staying in Pharr with Kells Elvins, it was time to jump the court case and go somewhere a man could be free: in October 1949 he moved to Mexico.

Burroughs took an apartment with Joan and the two children at 37 Cerrada de Medellín, Mexico City, and picked up his Mayan studies again at Mexico City College on the GI Bill ('always keep your snout in the public trough', he wrote to Kerouac[15]). Burroughs liked Mexico: 'In Mexico your wishes have a dream power. When you want to see someone, he turns up.'[16]

Life in Mexico was very laissez-faire about guns, drugs and boys. It was a relief to be rid of America, he wrote to Ginsberg, and to be in 'this fine, free country!' Freedom, along with a higher standard of living, was a quality Burroughs associated with the past: Mexico was 'where the US was in 1880 or so', so if Allen wanted a chance to get rich, and meanwhile live in 'a style that the US has not seen since 1914, "Go South of the Rio Grande, young man."' This complex of associations about the past gives rise to a characteristic image early in *The Soft Machine*: driving down to Mexico, 'the further South we went the easier it was to score like we brought the '20s along with us'.[17]

America had lost its 'glorious Frontier heritage of minding one's own business' but Mexico still had it: if a man wanted to wear a monocle or carry a cane, nobody cared. Young men could walk down the street arm in arm. A Mexican would never expect any criticism from a stranger, said Burroughs, nor would it ever occur to him to criticize anyone else.[18]

Burroughs had a recurrent bad dream about police authority – 'the recurrent cop of my dreams . . . who would rush in when I was about to take a shot or go to bed with a boy'[19] – but in Mexico even the police were inoffensive and useful public servants. They would never stop 'a well dressed upper class character' like himself[20] and he told Ginsberg that he had no fantasies of shooting them, unlike American cops.

He carried a gun all the time now, feeling not only unsafe but petit bourgeois without one. Joan, meanwhile, had developed theories that atomic radiation from bomb tests could function as a form of thought control. She was unable to get Benzedrine in Mexico, and she had started drinking tequila from eight in the morning. A brush with polio in New Orleans had left her weakened, with a limp, and the drink and drugs had given her a drab, ruined appearance.

Burroughs had taken up with boys again, and he frequented the queer bars the Ship Ahoy and the Green Lantern (the latter seemingly the Chimu Bar in *Junky*). He seems to have rented a second apartment to take them back to, including a steady Mexican boy called Angelo, picked up in the Chimu. Joan was tolerant about this, and when Burroughs wrote to Ginsberg and said that sex with women was like eating tortillas when you really wanted a steak, Joan added at the bottom of the letter 'Around the 20th of the month, things get a bit tight and he lives on tortillas.'[21]

Burroughs had made contact with the Mexico City junk scene, the subject of a memorable psychogeographical passage in *Junky*:

As the geologist looking for oil is guided by certain outcroppings of rock, so certain signs indicate the near presence of junk. Junk is often found adjacent to ambiguous or transitional districts: East Fourteenth near Third in New York; Poydras and St Charles in New Orleans; San Juan Letran on Mexico City. Stores selling artificial limbs, wig-makers, dental mechanics, loft manufacturers of perfumes, pomades, novelties, essential oils. A point where dubious business enterprise touches Skid Row.[22]

The Ace first edition of *Junkie* (1951).

Burroughs's supplies were ensured through a junky named Dave Tesorero (sometimes given as Tercerero, 'Old Ike' in *Junky*). After scoring via Tesorero from the woman who controlled the drug trade in Mexico City, Lola La Chata (something of a Salt Chunk Mary figure, 'Lupita' in *Junky*), Burroughs put up the money to keep Dave as a registered addict, and they split the supply.

Joan was not as tolerant about drugs as she was about boys, and she despaired. Burroughs was boring and listless when he was on junk, as if a light had gone off, and one day he was cooking up a shot in a spoon when she grabbed it and threw it away. He slapped her. This untypical moment is the source of the original

Junky cover, a generic piece of 1950s pulp art – it looks as if the woman is an unusually attractive dope fiend, being manfully restrained for her own good – showing a man and woman struggling over a hypodermic.

Burroughs intermittently tried to give up, but it usually led to drinking, which was worse. At one stage he developed incipient uraemic poisoning. He went though a bad patch early in 1951, getting drunk in public, bumping into trees, saying embarrassing things to strangers, and being disarmed after waving his gun around in bars. And as their friend Hal Chase remembered it, 'Joan was such a castrator . . . Bill was constantly being disarmed . . . And Joan would say, "So they took your gun away from you, did they?"' Even back in New York, Chase remembered, Joan had often been scornful of Burroughs: 'She'd describe in detail how he'd be all set to make love, and then he'd get cramp in his foot.'[23]

Burroughs and Joan loved each other but they were sick of each other too. There was a good deal of ambivalence in their relationship, particularly on Burroughs's side, and some time in autumn 1950 they had filed for divorce in Cuernavaca, a fact which later acquired a more sinister significance.

Burroughs was very interested in telepathy and the two of them would experiment with it, even in this sometimes difficult Mexico City period of their relationship. Lucien Carr, down on a visit, watched them each draw pictures on a sheet of paper divided into nine squares, then compare drawings. There seemed to be a remarkable degree of correlation – a scorpion, a bottle, a dog – and Carr found it uncanny. It was as if there was real telepathy between them, and he further felt that the stronger of the two, the broadcaster or sender, was Joan.[24]

Burroughs had earlier experimented telepathically with Kerouac, and he was convinced of its reality. There were great implications, as he told Ginsberg: these solid, demonstrable, verifiable facts pointed to the possibility of disembodied consciousness, and

fter death.[25] More than that, for Burroughs telepathy
nal aspiration. He writes repeatedly of communi-
pathy on a non-verbal level – again, amounting to
as the thing he looks for in human relations, and
notes its absence in the Panama civil service: 'You cannot contact
a civil servant on the level of intuition and empathy. He just does
not have a receiving set, and he gives out like a dead battery.'[27]

Burroughs had read of a South American drug which was said to
increase telepathy: this was yage (pronounced 'ya-hay'), *bannisteria
caapi*, from which the native drug ayahuasca was prepared. Its
active ingredient, harmaline, was then known as telepathine.
Burroughs ends *Junky* with the possibilities of yage compared
to junk – it may be the final fix, he says, 'the kick that opens out
instead of narrowing down' – ending the book on an expanding,
frontier note.

Yage was obscure but nevertheless still slightly 'in the air' in the
1950s. The Russians were said to be experimenting with yage as a
tool of mass-control for slave labour, and the CIA were interested
in rare plant hallucinogens including ayahuasca and mushrooms:
in June 1953 a CIA ARTICHOKE conference was told of drugs used by
Mexican witch doctors to find lost objects and predict the future; it
was 'essential', said the speaker, that the CIA should explore this.[28]

Just a few blocks from the flat on Cerrada de Medellin was
the Bounty Bar, popular with American students at Mexico City
College, and it was there around May 1951 that Burroughs had
met and fallen disastrously in love with an easygoing 21-year-old
American named Adelbert Lewis Marker. No intellectual, despite
his glasses giving him an owlish look, Marker had served in
Germany after the war with American Counter-Intelligence,
and he was now a student at MCC.

Marker was heterosexual but he liked Burroughs well enough,
particularly because he made him laugh, and Burroughs gives a
thinly novelized account of their relationship in his novel *Queer*,

where Marker figures as 'Eugene Allerton' (and, further blurring the line between fiction and autobiography, Burroughs refers to Marker as Allerton in his own despairing diary notebook of the time, now published as *Everything Lost*).

Burroughs was endlessly and desperately trying to beguile Marker by launching into comic flights of fancy, several of which turned into full-blown comic 'routines' such as 'Gus's Used Slave Lot', like a used car lot; the Texas oil men (with good ole boys like Fred Crockly and Roy Spigot); and finally the Skip Tracer, in which nobody escapes the Friendly Finance loan company. As Alan Ansen later wrote, the routines were essentially 'a Tom Sawyer handstand meant to impress'.[29]

Inevitably, much of Burroughs's desperate joking in *Queer* involves issues of manipulation, control, power and sexuality. He would never forget the 'unspeakable horror', he says – hamming it up for Allerton/Marker – 'when the baneful word seared my reeling brain: I was a homosexual. I thought of the painted, simpering female impersonators I had seen in a Baltimore night club. Could it be possible that I was one of those subhuman things? I might well have destroyed myself . . . Nobler, I thought, to die a man than live on, a sex monster . . .'.[30]

Burroughs asked Marker to accompany him on a two-man expedition into the Ecuadorian jungle in search of yage. Burroughs would pick up the tab for everything and keep him amused, and all Marker had to do was be his audience and consent to have sex with him twice a week as part of their contract.

Marker agreed, and they spent July to September 1951 travelling. It was a disaster. Burroughs's emotional needs were painful, however much he tried to joke about them. Marker liked to sleep alone, prompting 'Lee' to say that if he had his way they'd sleep all wrapped around each other like hibernating snakes. Prefiguring the desperate fusion Burroughs later called 'schlupping', Lee continues in baby talk: 'Wouldn't it be booful if we should juth run together into one gweat big blob . . . Am I giving you the horrors?' 'Indeed,' says Allerton, 'you are.'[31]

Burroughs sometimes felt sorry for Marker: 'He is such a child . . . he doesn't realize what he is involved in. Like the pity I felt for my severed finger, as if it was innocent victim of violent, unpredictable forces. Sometimes he looks hurt and puzzled, by the warped intensity of my emotions.'[32]

They found no yage, although they did find a tough old botanist named Fuller ('Cotter' in *Queer*) who lived in the jungle with his wife and had contact with the Indians. He told them ayahuasca was connected to *brujeria*, witchcraft, and that he could introduce them to a *brujo*, but Burroughs saw he didn't really want to. After three days they left, with Fuller making little effort to conceal his relief, and Burroughs returned in defeat to Mexico City.

He continued to nurse his obsession with Marker, and later ruminated on the significance of his comic routines as a tactic to charm him. He was attempting black magic, he said.

> Black magic is always an attempt to force human love, resorted to when there is no other way to score. (Even curse is last attempt at contact with loved one. I do not contemplate any curse, that is absolute end of wrong line. . . . The curse is a last attempt to regain attention.) I want his love, but even more I want he should recognise my love for him. By indifference he cuts me off from expressing life, from my way of expressing life, from life itself. In short I am aware of wanting human love.[33]

He explored it from a slightly different angle in a later poem, 'To M.', which he probably never sent to Marker but showed to Ginsberg. Now his love was seen in terms of addiction and withdrawal sickness, or the gutting wound of a dum-dum bullet. Finally, he writes:

Please don't hurt me so I can't help wanting to hurt you.
At least wish me luck.
And let me stay ready to help you any way I can.

He added a despairing postscript to Ginsberg, saying Marker wouldn't even wish him luck or say goodbye.[34]

Burroughs's sadness over Marker had meanwhile been compounded with another grief. On the sixth of September 1951 Burroughs heard the fluting whistle of an itinerant knife grinder, and he went out to get a knife sharpened. It was a Scout knife he had bought in Quito while travelling with Marker. As Burroughs walked towards the knife grinder's cart he was suddenly overcome by intense feelings of despair, loss and doom, and tears began to stream down his face.

5

A Slip of the Gun

With hindsight the music of the knife grinder, the weeping, and an event as yet to happen all crystallize together like an epiphany, but at the time the music – and the knife – probably evoked his recent travels, plunging him back into the unhappy situation with Marker.

Burroughs had heard something like the grinder's melancholy music before – it is traditionally a simple scale played up and down on a pan pipe – first when he was in Albania in the 1930s, and then repeatedly in South America: in *The Yage Letters* he plays it on a jukebox ('archaic . . . strangely familiar, very old and very sad'); in *Queer* he sees it played in a market, by a hunchback with withered legs; and in a South American notebook it figures with a dream of a great atomic cloud,

> spreading a purple black shadow . . . darker and darker . . . The Chinamen are shutting the doors of their shops, pulling down metal blinds.
> A blind legless beggar plays a sad high mountain tune on a bamboo pipe in the empty street.[1]

Significantly, all these encounters with the music are *written* – whenever they happen biographically – *after* the shooting of Joan, and perhaps emotionally inflected by it.

Burroughs collected himself enough to hand his knife over for sharpening. Years later he wondered what became of it, because as events fell out it was never reclaimed. He returned and started knocking back drinks with Joan in the Bounty Bar. He was low on money, he had a pistol he wanted to sell, a Star .38 automatic, and in the early evening he was due to meet the potential buyer – someone known to the Bounty's co-owner, John Healy, whom Burroughs was friendly with – in a flat above the bar.

Bill and Joan went up, Billy Junior with them, to find the buyer hadn't arrived but Marker and his friend Eddie Woods were there, drinking. Accounts of what happened next vary. He seems to have said to Joan 'I guess it's about time for our William Tell act.' Joan was fairly drunk and she giggled as she balanced a glass on her head.

Burroughs took aim at the the top of the glass and fired, with the shocking sound of a gun indoors. A moment later the glass was on the floor, but still unbroken. Joan's head had tilted, and then Marker said 'Bill, I think you hit her.' 'No!' cried Burroughs, and leapt up to sit across Joan's lap and hold her, saying, 'Joan, Joan, Joan!'[2]

There was a small blue hole in Joan's forehead, four or five centimetres to the left of the centre. Mercifully there was no exit wound. Then blood began to trickle out. Joan subsided slightly with a snoring sound. This was mistaken by one or two people present for a 'death rattle', although in fact she didn't die until after she reached hospital.

Over the years, as James Campbell has noted, the object on Joan's head has been reported as a highball glass, a champagne glass, a whiskey glass, an apricot, an orange, an apple, a full glass of gin, a six-ounce water glass, a wine glass and a tin can. Their son Billy Jr, then four, later wrote 'she placed an apple or an apricot or a grape or myself on her head and challenged my father to shoot.'[3]

Hal Chase, who wasn't there, said it had been deliberate murder. Eddie Woods, who was, conceded there just might have been some murderous impulse, unconsciously, but *really* unconsciously . . .

Heir's Pistol Kills His Wife; He Denies Playing Wm. Tell

Mexico City, Sept. 7 (*AP*).—William Seward Burroughs, 37, first admitted, then denied today that he was playing William Tell when his gun killed his pretty, young wife during a drinking party last night.

Police said that Burroughs, grandson of the adding machine inventor, first told them that, wanting to show off his marksmanship, he placed a glass of gin on her head and fired, but was so drunk that he missed and shot her in the forehead.

After talking with a lawyer, police said, Burroughs, who is a wealthy cotton planter from Pharr, Tex., changed his story and insisted that his wife was shot accidentally when he dropped his newly-purchased .38 caliber pistol.

Husband in Jail.

Mrs. Burroughs, 27, the former Joan Vollmer, died in the Red Cross Hospital.

The shooting occurred during a party in the apartment of John Healy of Minneapolis. Burroughs said two other American tourists whom he knew only slightly were present.

Burroughs, hair disheveled and clothes wrinkled, was in jail today. A hearing on a charge of homicide is scheduled for tomorrow morning.

No Arguments, He Says.

"It was purely accidental," he said. "I did not put any glass on her head. If she did, it was a joke. I certainly did not intend to shoot at it."

He said there had been no arguments or discussion before the "accident."

"The party was quiet," he said. "We had a few drinks. Everything is very hazy."

Burroughs and his wife had been here about two years. He said he was studying native dialects at the University of Mexico. He explained his long absence from his ranch by saying that he was unsuited for business.

Wife From Albany.

He said he was born in St. Louis and that his wife was from Albany, N. Y. They have two children, William Burroughs Jr., 3, and

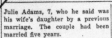

William Seward Burroughs in Mexico City prison.

(Associated Press Wirefotos)
The late Mrs. Joan Burroughs— killed at party.

Julie Adams, 7, who he said was his wife's daughter by a previous marriage. The couple had been married five years.

She had attended journalism school at Columbia University before her marriage to Burroughs. Burroughs, who also had been married before, formerly lived in

Loudonville, a swank suburb of Albany. He is a graduate of Harvard University and worked for two weeks in 1942 as a reporter for the St. Louis Post-Dispatch.

His paternal grandfather laid the foundation of a fortune when he built his first adding machine in St. Louis in 1885.

'Heir's Pistol Kills His Wife': *New York Daily News*, 8 September 1951.

I remember it so vividly, his shock'.[4] Joan was taken to hospital and Burroughs to the police station. While Burroughs was talking to a police officer, word came from the hospital that the wounded woman had died. Burroughs cried, tearing his hair.

Burroughs had already had some contact with a high-powered Mexican lawyer, Bernabe Jurado, over his problems with settling in Mexico (these immigration difficulties had meanwhile tempered his initially sunny view of the place). Now he needed him as never before, and years later he remembered him as 'My Most Unforgettable Character':

> Right here I step into a universe of smiley corruption. And here is The Man himself. He puts his pearl-handled .45 auto on a table. He is 6'3', broad shoulders. As a clerk in his office said, 'What a man.'[5]

Jurado immediately made Burroughs change his story. Burroughs had already told the police about the William Tell act, but now it seemed he had been examining the gun, and showing his friends how it worked, when suddenly it slipped and fired.

Burroughs was detained in Mexico City's 'Black Palace of Lecumberri' prison, but Jurado got him out on bail after thirteen days. Burroughs's family were on hand with any money that was needed, and a widespread view of the case is represented by Ted Morgan's comment that 'the pillars of the Mexican justice system were bribery and perjury'.[6] In fact there is every indication that the Mexican court was highly sensitive to this reputation, and that Burroughs's trial was a fair one, swallowing Jurado's lie but nevertheless coming to the correct verdict that it was an accidental tragedy. A year later, having been on bail in the meantime, Burroughs was sentenced to two years suspended, minus thirteen days. Burroughs was impressed by the straightforward decency of the Mexicans who dealt with him during his ordeal.

The court may have been honest but Jurado was not, and it is likely that the money Burroughs and his family handed over in order to – for example – 'bribe ballistics experts' in fact went no further than Jurado himself. Years later Jurado boasted of meeting Burroughs again in Casablanca and frightening him into handing over a further $20,000 to stay free; a highly unlikely story.

It was in Jurado's office that Burroughs had first met Dave Tesorero, and Jurado himself offered Burroughs an ounce of heroin for $500. Jurado took cocaine before his court performances but he wasn't interested in heroin, and said he knew nothing about it. In the event Burroughs let Bill Garver have it instead, but there was something not right with it: Garver became delirious, and for a while Burroughs thought he might die.

Billy Jr had a clear memory from a few weeks later of his daddy taking him to a fountain pond in a Mexico City park, before he went away to live with his grandparents. Burroughs had a very special present for him, a red boat that ran on real fire from methylated spirits soaked into cotton wool. '"We have to be careful now," he said with the utmost gravity as he shakily lit the cotton and then the little boat chugged crazy circles on the water.'[7]

The moment was spoiled for Billy by some greasy-haired youths watching them and sniggering. He was afraid. Years later the whole business seemed like a further instance of what he thought of as The Burroughs Curse. 'I don't know when it was first visited upon us, but I felt it then and the chug, chug, snicker, snicker painted a very lasting picture.'[8]

Joan had been buried quietly at the American Cemetery, or *Panteon Americano*. Meanwhile, as she lay in the hospital morgue, an unknown hand had placed a Mexican saint's pendant on her as a blessing. Ginsberg later dreamed of her, asking after their old friends and telling him she'd gone on to find 'new loves in the west'.[9]

Burroughs never stopped turning the event over in his mind. He even thought of trying to write something about it, but he couldn't bring himself to do it. He was afraid, he wrote in a 1954 letter with his most morbid and uncanny take on the event, not so much of finding an 'unconscious intent' but something altogether weirder, as if the brain had somehow drawn the bullet towards it.[10]

Otherwise his feelings circled around guilt, hidden culpabilities and unknown agencies. Perhaps, in the coincidental but all too apposite perception of his old analyst, Dr Federn, years earlier, in addition to slips of the hand and slips of the tongue, we must now add *slips of the gun*.[11]

Burroughs came to feel he had been possessed by an evil spirit when he shot Joan, something he knew not everyone would accept. Forty-five years later he wrote in his journal 'What they really can't understand is *division, possession* . . . Tell any feminist I shot Joan in a state of possession, and she will scream: 'Nonsense! No such thing. HE did it.'[12] Looking back, he wrote,

> I am forced to the appalling conclusion that I would never
> have become a writer but for Joan's death . . . I live with the
> constant threat of possession, and a constant need to escape
> from possession, from Control. So the death of Joan brought
> me in contact with the invader, the Ugly Spirit, and manoeu-
> vered me into a lifelong struggle, in which I have had no
> choice except to write myself out.[13]

In this construction it was a decisive event, solidifying Burroughs's pre-Enlightenment sense of the self as subject to possession, more medieval than Freudian, but in literal terms of his writing career it is disingenuous. Juvenilia aside, he'd already worked on 'Twilight's Last Gleamings' with Elvins and 'Hippos' with Kerouac, and since early 1950 he had been writing an account of his experiences with junk, encouraged by Ginsberg and Kells Elvins (who had moved to Mexico City with his wife in order to study psychology with Erich Fromm at the Medical School there).

Burroughs had difficulties finding a publisher for *Junky*, his extraordinary first book. It could have been written by no one else. Consider the way in which his account of those 'ambiguous or transitional' junk districts suddenly slides to describe a mysterious figure, eastern and probably Egyptian, supposedly seen nearby:

He is basically obscene beyond any possible vile act or practice. He has the mark of a certain trade or occupation that no longer exists . . .

So this man walks around in the places where he once exercised his obsolete and unthinkable trade. But he is unperturbed. His eyes are black with an insect's unseeing calm. He looks as if he nourished himself on honey and Levantine syrups that he sucks up through a sort of proboscis.

What is his lost trade? Definitely of a servant class and something to do with the dead, although he is not an embalmer. Perhaps he stores something in his body – a substance to prolong life – of which he is periodically milked by his masters. He is as specialized as an insect, for the performance of some inconceivably vile function.[14]

No, said a senior editor at Doubleday; 'This could only work if it was written by someone important, like Winston Churchill.'[15]

Ginsberg finally managed to place *Junky* through a friend he'd met during a spell in psychiatric hospital, Carl Solomon. Solomon's uncle, A. A. Wyn, ran the sensationalist paperback house of Ace Books, and Solomon had a job there. Having finished *Junky*, Burroughs began a sequel about his trip to Peru with Marker, provisionally entitled *Queer*. It is a very different book to *Junky*. Where *Junky* – completed before Joan's death – is written in the first person and has the cool, hipster calm of Burroughs on junk,

Queer is written in the third person as the study of a vulnerable and unhappy man (the death of Joan remains entirely offstage and unmentioned) who is off drugs, emotionally desperate and falling to pieces with unrequited love.

In the event *Queer* stayed unpublished until 1985, although Ace were originally interested in the two books together, leading to further irritations. At one moment, almost too good to be true, Solomon seems to have wanted to title the book *Fag.* 'Now look,' Burroughs wrote to Ginsberg in April 1952,

> You tell Solomon I don't mind being called queer. T. E. Lawrence and all manner of right Joes (boy can I turn a phrase) was queer. But I'll see him castrated before I'll be called a Fag. That's just what I was trying to put down uh I mean *over*, is the distinction between us strong, manly, noble types and the leaping, jumping, window dressing cocksucker. Furthechrissakes a girl's gotta draw the line somewheres or publishers will swarm all over her sticking their nasty old biographical prefaces up her ass.[16]

Later in 1952 Burroughs's lying thug of a lawyer was driving along in his fishtail Cadillac when he had a very minor accident with another car driven by a seventeen-year-old boy, and Jurado shot him. It was a minor wound, but after the boy developed tetanus and died Jurado skipped the country.

With his protector gone, Jurado's law office started trying to extort more money from Burroughs, and he decided to follow Jurado's example and get out. In December 1952 he took off for the us by car with an acquaintance named Tex Riddle (aka 'Tex the Trotskyite') who was wanted for 'paper hanging', or writing dud cheques. Tex suggested they should rob a bank and then lie low in Bolivia, but Burroughs thought not, and he spent Christmas 1953 safely at his parent's house, reunited with Billy Jr.

It transpired that Ace were now planning to publish *Junky* bound back-to-back as an 'Ace Double' with the memoirs of a federal narcotics agent, but Burroughs was past caring. He was determined to go to the jungle again, continuing the quest for yage, and in January 1953 he went down to Panama, where Bill Garver was taking advantage of the easy supply of paregoric. Garver suggested they should go into pig farming down there and Burroughs imagined the two of them as farmers, with Garver sitting out on the veranda all day, semi-conscious.

Burroughs had a painful operation for piles at the American Hospital in Panama, and the spell in hospital was another impetus for yet another of his regular attempts to get off junk. He had an ambivalence to it, unlike Garver, and he wrote to Ginsberg saying how much better he felt without it. This time there would be no stopping him in the quest for yage, or ayahuasca, or telepathine: 'the uncut kick', as he had written at the end of *Junky*, 'that opens out instead of narrowing down like junk'.

From Panama Burroughs went to Bogotá and on down the Putumayo river, between Colombia and Ecuador. His South American travels (Colombia, Ecuador, Bolivia, Peru) were summarized by Ginsberg later – 'Jungles and end-of-road Conradian despair in mudhut Bolivian towns. He went there to experiment with native magic and drugs, kind of an Ahab quest'[17] – and Burroughs used his impressions in *The Yage Letters*, full of jaundiced black humour, some haunting travel writing, and his trademark hyperboles, sometimes extreme and sometimes more subtle, like his faintly surreal account of the botanical department of Colombia university at Bogotá. There were locked, unlabelled offices and dusty corridors, where he had to climb over packing crates and botanical presses and stuffed animals:

These articles are continually being moved from one room to another for no discernible reason. People rush out of offices and claim some object from the litter in the hall and have it carried back into their offices. The porters sit around on crates smoking and greeting everybody as 'Doctor'.[18]

It was here that he met Richard Schultes ('Doc Schindler' in *The Yage Letters*), another old Harvard man and a legendary authority on hallucinogenic plants.

Burroughs travelled to Mocoa and on to Puerto Limon, where he found an old brujo who prepared a cold water infusion of yage. At first Burroughs found it to be a rougher route to a cannabis-type experience, including aphrodisiac effects and anxiety. Subsequent experiences convinced him it could be nauseating, frightening stuff, and that it was wise to have tranquilizing Nembutal to hand, but still the results were inconclusive.

At one point he had a vision of a city, which was traditional with yage: the Indians reported seeing cities. Burroughs seems to have read this in a men's magazine article, a characteristic source, and he wrote the article into an unused account of his experiences, part memory and part skit, where a Danish explorer reports a Medicine Man who, 'under the effects of yage, described in detail the business district of Copenhagen, even writing out street signs though in a normal state he was illiterate'.[19]

Burroughs ran into trouble with an error on his tourist card, dated 1952 instead of 1953 by the Colombian consul, and was detained by the local police in Puerto Assis and then Mocoa. This was only one of his troubles; he was also beset by malarial parasites, petty thieving and post-surgical problems. Doctors were 'croakers' in the slang of Burroughs's circle, and he complained to Ginsberg 'that fucking croaker in Panama bungled my ass'.[20]

Burroughs had to return to Bogotá, still determined to go back to the jungle. Schultes now gave him a decisive break, getting him attached in a vague capacity to an expedition with the Cocoa Commission (the Anglo-Colombian Cacao Expedition). One of

In search of yage: Burroughs in the Colombian jungle, 1953.

the Englishmen, Paul Holliday, recorded him as 'A tall lank, droopy sort of person with a pessimistic streak for conjuring up all manner of fearful fevers one can collect around Putumayo; a pleasant fellow though, talkative and dryly amusing.' Burroughs had never been to Britain and he observed the Brits in turn, with one of them saying to him – about the Colombian plant gatherers on the expedition – 'So long as they can collect any old weed they don't give a ruddy fuck.'[21]

Burroughs was changing. His politics were mellowing; he stopped using 'Liberal' as a term of abuse in South America, noticing that South American conservatives were a thoroughly ugly bunch and that intelligent, sympatico people down there were invariably Liberals. His comic talents were sharpening, and while he was on this second Yage expedition he posted a letter to Ginsberg, dated 23 May 1953, containing his first full-blown written 'routine' – he still calls it a 'skit' at this stage – 'Roosevelt After Inauguration'.

It has little to do with the real Roosevelt, but it imagines a fantastically corrupt President installing his low-life cronies to State positions, appointing a Turkish bath attendant as head of the FBI, and forcing the members of the Supreme Court to be sodomized by a purple-assed baboon. The new government then institutes Turn In Your Best Friend Week, Molest a Child Week, and a competition for the title of All-Around Vilest Man of the Year.

'Roosevelt was convulsed with such hate for the human species as it is, that he wished to degrade it beyond recognition', writes Burroughs, and the piece ends with Roosevelt gazing at the sky: '"I'll make the cocksuckers glad to mutate," he would say, looking off into space as if seeking new frontiers of depravity.'[22] It immediately ran into legal trouble when it was published a few years later.

Finally, in June and July 1953, Burroughs had the full yage experience. It transpired that the cold water infusion was not enough, and that it needed the addition of two other plants to activate it. He wrote to Ginsberg on 18 June that yage was not like cannabis after all, nor anything else. The night before, he had experienced extraordinary things, almost indescribable: he could paint it, he said, if only he could paint. He had felt himself possessed by a blue spirit, with an air of the South Pacific – Easter Island or Maori – and a grinning archaic face. He also felt intensely sexual, in this instance heterosexual.

By 8 July he had been further, with five or so trips. The room had taken the aspect of a Near Eastern whorehouse, with blue walls and red tasselled lamps. The beautiful blue substance was flowing, and the archaic grinning face was blue splotched with gold. Burroughs felt his long, awkward, ectomorphic legs growing more rounded, with a Polynesian quality. He turned into a black woman. The room was at once Near Eastern, and Polynesian, and

Paul Klee's 1935 watercolour drawing *Indiscretion*: an 'exact copy of what I saw high on yage in Pucallpa when I closed my eyes', Burroughs told Ginsberg.

yet oddly familiar. Everything seemed to writhe with a peculiar furtive life. In lighter intoxication the ambience seemed Eastern, but with deeper intoxication it grew more South Pacific.[23]

Yage, said Burroughs, was space-time travel. And perhaps that was why it was initially nauseating: the preliminary yage nausea was actually the 'motion sickness' of being transported to the yage state. Burroughs remembered that H. G. Wells – an underrated writer, he felt – had written of the indescribable vertigo of space-time travel in *The Time Machine*.[24]

Trying to describe what he had been through, Burroughs mentions at least three times that he wishes he could paint it.[25] He admired the work of Paul Klee, whose pictures seemed autonomously alive, and Klee reminded him of yage, one picture in particular: '*Indiscretion* is exact copy of what I saw high on yage in Pucallpa when I closed my eyes'.[26] This picture had been at the Bucholz Galleries, New York, in 1938, but it is more likely Burroughs knew it from Daniel-Henry Kahnweiler's monograph *Klee* (Paris, 1950) where it is reproduced in colour. Painted in 1935, and predominantly ochre or reddish brown against a dark back-ground, it features a jumble of heavy curving forms – almost gut-like or muscular, with a sense of some unknown night-time convolution – and what looks like a face lurking behind them to one side, like a suspended ghostly presence.

Another important comparison to the yage experience, for Burroughs, was the work of French poet Saint-John Perse (1887–1975). 'St Perse. *This is Yage. Poetry.*' Burroughs wrote in a South American notebook.[27] Perse is not only an extraordinary writer ('Tattooers of exiled Queens and cradlers of moribund monkeys in the basements of great hotels, / Radiologists helmeted with lead on the edge of betrothal beds, / And sponge-fishermen in green waters, brushing by marble girls and latin bronzes, / The story tellers in the forest . . .') but there is something strongly akin to Burroughs in his plural generalities and delirious catalogues:

Burroughs reading Saint-John Perse in Ginsberg's apartment, September 1953, photographed by Ginsberg.

With foam on their lips and claws held high, the migrations of crabs over the earth march across old coastal plantations boarded up for the winter like disabled Federal batteries. Brown cockroaches are in the music rooms and the granary; black serpents coiled on the linens' freshness in the camphor and cypress laundries.

In the morning the black roses of Opera Singers floated down the rivers soiled with dawn, in the yellow-reds of alcohol and opium. And the iron gates of the Widows, in deserted patios, raised in vain against time their white coral portcullis.

... the galleries of laterite, the vestibules of black stone and the pools of clear shadow for libraries; cool places for the chemical products ... And already in the streets a man sang alone, one of those who paint on their brow the cipher of their god. (Perpetual crackling of insects in this quarter of vacant lots and rubbish) ...[28]

The substance and style of Perse's most famous work, *Anabasis*, is well caught in 'Migrations, incredible journeys through deserts and jungles and mountains', although it is a line from Burroughs describing the yage state.[29]

Burroughs was reading Perse's *Vents*, published in translation that year as *Wind*, in Ginsberg's apartment late in 1953, and had already given Perse's *Anabasis* to Ginsberg as a present.[30] It seems to be the mixed influence of taking yage and reading Saint-John Perse that set Burroughs up to write 'the City' at the end of *The Yage Letters*:

> Minarets, palms, mountains, jungle . . . vast weed grown parks where boys lie in the grass or play cryptic games . . . Tables and booths, and bars and rooms and kitchens and baths, copulating couples on rows of brass beds, criss cross of a thousand hammocks, junkies tying up, opium smokers, hashish smokers . . . gaming tables where the games are played for incredible stakes . . . All houses in the City are joined. Houses of sod with high mountain Mongols blinking in smoky doorways, houses of bamboo and teak wood . . . South Pacific and Maori houses, houses in trees and houses on river boats . . . great rusty iron racks rising 200 feet in the air from swamps and rubbish with perilous partitions built on multileveled platforms and hammocks swinging over the void.
>
> Expeditions leave for unknown places with unknown purpose . . . High mountain flutes and jazz and bebop and one stringed Mongol instruments . . . . the untended dead are eaten by vultures in the street . . . Albinos blink in the sun, boys sit in trees languidly masturbating . . . diseased beggars live in a maze of burrows under the city and pop out anywhere often pushing up through the floor of a crowded cafe.
>
> Followers of obsolete unthinkable trades doodling in Etruscan, addicts of drugs not yet synthesised . . . black

marketeers of World War III, pitchmen selling remedies for radiation sickness, investigators of infractions denounced by bland paranoid chess players . . . sellers of orgone tanks and relaxing machines, brokers of exquisite dreams and memories tested on the sensitized cells of junk sickness . . .[31]

In summer 1953 Burroughs returned briefly to Mexico City. He felt as if he had been away for years, not months. Everyone seemed to be long gone: Joan and little Billy, Dave the junky, Jurado, Angelo and Marker.

Back after his quest for yage, Burroughs felt like an unwanted Captain Ahab, as if he had returned from pursuing Moby Dick only to find his wife and mistress had both deserted him for other men and nobody even wanted to hear about what he had been through: 'Sure, Jack, the white whale . . . yeah . . . Scuse me I got like an appointment.'[32]

He missed Angelo, the Mexican boy. He could visualize him so acutely in his green jumper, 'sharp and clear as [an] overdue pusher'. He remembered how free from hostility and sweet-natured he was, 'sweet and sad . . . The way he used to help around the [apartment] and he hoped I would help him, and now I want to and he is gone.'[33]

He asked around after Marker and learned he had been around until relatively recently. It was like an injection of pure desolation, 'a cold spreading misery that settles in the lungs and around the heart.' He must have received Burroughs's letters. 'Why didn't he answer Why?'[34] Burroughs didn't want to let Marker go, and the last of the comic routines he dreamed up for him was the Skip Tracer, painfully close to the truth: Burroughs's unwelcome pursuit was so persistent it was now comparable to the long arm of Friendly Finance.

He had a dream in which Marker had been away and asking questions about yage, which was doubly comforting: he wanted to help with information, and being away explained why he hadn't written. But in waking reality Burroughs was bereft: the South American trip had not only been gruelling in itself, but it was 'a disaster that lost me everything I had of value. Bits of it keep floating back to me like memories of a day time nightmare.' 'Everything lost', he wrote, and (quoting Lady Macbeth) 'Nought's had, all's spent.'[35]

Burroughs cut his losses and left Mexico City in August 1953. He went briefly to his parents' house in Palm Beach before going on to stay with Ginsberg for three months in New York. *Junky* had just been published (as *Junkie*) and sold over 100,000 copies in its first year without receiving a single review, although it was much admired by Ginsberg and also Kerouac, who offered a slightly bizarre (and in the event unused) blurb, describing it as the work of a 'learned, vicious, Goering-like sophisticate'.[36] Burroughs was at least pleased to find that Maurice Helbrandt, the narcotics agent whose book it was double-bound with, seemed less obnoxious than he expected.

Staying with Ginsberg, Burroughs worked on *The Yage Letters* with Ginsberg's help. This fictionalized version of his South American travels reads deceptively like real letters, but it was re-cast into epistolary form from a draft of solid prose. The yage experience, rendered as a flowing Perse-style vision of place, became the germ of *Naked Lunch*. 'Originally,' Ginsberg says in a 1992 dialogue between two eminent old writers,

Interzone and The Market [key sections of *Lunch*] had their origins in notes you wrote when we were editing *The Yage Letters* together in late 1953. I always thought the Interzone Meet Cafe was the seed of *Naked Lunch*.

'Absolutely,' says Burroughs. 'Yes.'[37]

Aspects of Interzone were further hyperbolized, in a delirious, dreamlike form, from the landscape around Ginsberg's flat, as

Ginsberg's photo of Burroughs and the sphinx, Metropolitan Museum, New York, autumn 1953.

Barry Miles has noted:

> The futuristic vibrating city of Interzone, with its levels connected by a web of catwalks, was inspired by the fire escapes and washing lines in Allen's back yard . . . Fire escapes faced each other across the back-yard courtyards, with washing lines going from building to building: level upon level of apartment fire escapes and laundry lines all connected. Bill conceived of a futuristic city made up of catwalks, boardwalks and fire escapes; a great labyrinth of alleyways and hallways; a city so old that it had been rebuilt layer upon layer . . .[38]

It was also at this time, seemingly through Ginsberg, that Burroughs's various 'gags', 'skits' and 'sketches' were re-labelled with their definitive identity as 'routines'. The two of them collaborated closely, and the emotional intensity that Burroughs had sought in Marker, a desire to merge with the other person, was now transferred to Ginsberg and accompanied by the new label of 'schlupping'. Burroughs wanted the two of them to 'schlupp' together into one symbiotic being, a longing later given ridiculous and repulsive form in a *Naked Lunch* routine about narcotics agent Bradley the Buyer ('Schlup . . . schlup schlup'), who finally has to be destroyed with a flamethrower.

Ginsberg and Burroughs were now in a sexual relationship, although the older man – 39 to Ginsberg's 27 – wasn't Ginsberg's type. And, in the words of Ted Morgan, Ginsberg found sex with Burroughs 'too bizarre to be satisfying. For Burroughs in the act of sex underwent an amazing transformation. This reserved, sardonic, masculine man became a gushing, ecstatic, passionate woman. The change was so extreme and startling that Allen was alarmed . . . He seemed to melt completely, to take on a different identity, as he had in narcoanalysis with Dr Wolberg, to become some recognizable female type . . . mushily romantic, vulnerably whimpering . . . '.[39]

In Ginsberg's words, Burroughs had 'a soft centre', and with his schlupping he wanted nothing less than 'an ultimate telepathic union of souls'. Suddenly Ginsberg couldn't stand it, and he blurted out 'I don't want your ugly old cock.' 'It wounded him terribly', he recalled later, ' . . . like complete physical rejection in a way I didn't mean. Like a heart blow . . . I'd freaked out for that moment and regretted it ever since.'[40]

For some time Burroughs had been meaning to go to Tangier, and he left New York at the start of December 1953. He left his home-made 'orgone accumulator' box in Ginsberg's flat, looking suddenly ridiculous and a little pathetic.

Burroughs went to Tangier via Rome, which he visited with Alan Ansen, a former secretary to W. H. Auden. According to Ansen, after reading Gore Vidal's *The Judgment of Paris* Burroughs intended to 'steep himself in vice'[41] in Rome, but he found it disappointing and cold. His character armour was back in place, at least most of the time. Ansen was moved by Rome in a way that Burroughs largely wasn't, and he particularly loved the fountains. He wrote to Ginsberg that the Trevi Fountain was so wonderful, 'even old Cactus Boy melted'.[42]

6

Tangier and *Naked Lunch*

For Burroughs the attraction of Tangier could be put in one word: 'exemption. Exemption from interference . . . Your private life is your own, to act exactly as you please.'[1] He arrived in January 1954 and took up lodging at 1 Calle de los Arcos, near the Socco Chico, a male brothel run by a man named Anthony Reithorst and known as 'Dutch Tony's'.

Paul Bowles, doyen of the literary scene in Tangier, has written:

If I said that Tangier struck me as a dream city, I should mean it in the strict sense. Its topography is rich in prototypal dream scenes: covered streets like corridors with doors opening into rooms on each side, hidden terraces high above the sea, streets consisting only of steps, dark impasses, small squares built on sloping terrain so that they looked like ballet sets designed in false perspective, with alleys leading off in several directions; as well as the classical dream equipment of tunnels, ramparts, ruins and cliffs.[2]

Burroughs found something similar, with a further twist of his own: Tangier seemed to exist on 'several dimensions', so the walker could always find streets, parks and squares that they had never seen before. It was a place where 'fact merges into dream, and dreams erupt into the real world.'[3]

Burroughs missed Ginsberg badly, as he confided to Kerouac. Ginsberg wasn't writing letters, and Burroughs wrote to Kerouac in April 1954 that he hadn't known he was 'hooked on him like this.

The withdrawal symptoms are worse than the Marker habit. One letter would fix me . . .'.[4]

Burroughs was meanwhile getting fixed in Tangier with an exceptionally addictive opiate called Eukodol, or dolophine (named after the Führer, this had been manufactured by the Germans as a wartime painkiller and the world now had surplus stocks). It could be bought over the counter in Tangier, and it led Burroughs to a rock-bottom habit.

Kerouac was interested in Buddhism, as Burroughs had been: he had already told Kerouac how interesting Tibetan Buddhism was, advising him to 'dig it', but Burroughs now disavowed it. He felt that for many people Buddhism could be a form of 'psychic junk', and said his present position was now the opposite:

> We are here in human form to learn by the human hiero-glyphs of love and suffering. There is no intensity of love or feeling that does not involve the risk of crippling hurt. It is a duty to take this risk, to love and feel without defence or reserve.[5]

Burroughs also advised Kerouac not to give up on sex, which he said he had lost interest in and no longer enjoyed.

Burroughs' own sexual life improved when he met a Spanish boy, 'Kiki' Enrique or Henrique, who became his regular casual partner for the next couple of years. There was no serious conversation and he was no substitute for Ginsberg, but at least Burroughs had the philosophical serenity of sexual satisfaction, as he wrote to Kerouac, adding that he also had 'the Wisdom of the East' in the 'streamlined' form of his dolophine.[6]

Burroughs turned 40 in Tangier and his life was in a crisis, personally and professionally. He was living off his parents, he had barely had a real job for more than a few months, he had published

Burroughs and 'Kiki' Enrique in Tangier, 1954, photographed by Ginsberg.

one book to no reviews, and he felt socially isolated and unloved. He was always knocking himself out for his friends, he said, and

> they dismiss me as a vampire who tries to buy them with some gift, money, or routines, or cut off fingers. Even if I lost my life in service of a friend, he would likely say: 'Oh he is trying to buy me with his ugly old life.'[7]

'Failure is mystery', he wrote in 'Lee's Journals'; 'A man does not mesh somehow with time-place.' He could have been successful, he thought – as a criminal, a psychoanalyst, a business executive, a drug trafficker, an anthropologist, an explorer, even a bullfighter – but the circumstances had never been there and instead he moved through the world 'like a ghost'. He felt a sort of horror, a premonition of 'deterioration and failure and final loneliness', with his future self 'just a crazy old bore somewhere in a bar with my routines'.[8]

Burroughs had no contact with Tangier high society, the world of Woolworth's heiress Barbara Hutton and expat English aristocrat and social arbiter David Herbert ('Queen of Tangier'). There was no writers' colony either, or if there was it was hiding from him. He felt ignored by the likes of Paul and Jane Bowles (subjects of a comic routine in one of his letters: 'Miggles looked up at her husband. She sniffed sharply: "Have you been rolling in carrion again?"[9]).

Bowles invited Tangier's 'dreariest queens' to tea, Burroughs complained to Kerouac, but he never invited him. Bowles and the painter Brion Gysin and various other cultural figures seemed to want nothing to do with him, and he felt they had sent him to Coventry.[10]

This was largely in Burroughs's mind, and when he finally got to know Bowles he found him immensely *sympathique*. This was even more true of Brion Gysin, whose spell he would later fall under in Paris, despite having had some very sharp perceptions of him in Tangier. Gysin was a gossip, a 'paranoid bitch on wheels', and a man who tried to cut Burroughs socially: Burroughs had managed not to 'see' Gysin, he reported, so Gysin didn't have a chance to blank him (he was 'learning the practices of this dreary tribe'.) Moreover Gysin had a snobbery which was perfectly suited to his career as a restaurateur running his 1001 Nights restaurant, and depicted by Burroughs as 'Algren':

As a fashionable restaurateur, Algren is superb, just the correct frequency of glacial geniality [. . .] 'Last night the coatroom was stacked with mink. There's a lot of money in [Tangier]', he says. . . . A rich old woman put up the loot. Algren doesn't have dime one, but he's a character who will get rich by acting like he is rich already. And Algren is crazy in a way that will help. He has a paranoid conceit. He is a man who never has one good word to say for anybody, and that's the way a man should be to run a fashionable night spot. Everyone will want to be the exception, the one person he really likes.[11]

Instead of Tangier high society, Burroughs was condemned to its teeming world of washed up drifters, oddballs, mooches and outsiders, brilliantly recorded in his 'International Zone'. He knew the English gangster Paul Lund, and in the shape of an Australian journalist named George Greaves he found what he thought was the most completely corrupt man he had ever encountered: Burroughs liked to imitate him saying 'You have to take a broad, general view of things.'[12]

Burroughs also befriended an English public school man named Eric Gifford, who seemed to have failed at everything and to be fantastically unlucky. He was the type of man who gets involved in fur farming or raising frogs, Burroughs thought,[13] and he had lost his savings in a bee-farming venture. His medical and sexual misadventures were little better, and he was the inspiration for the 'Leif the Unlucky' routine in *Naked Lunch*. Gifford became involved with stolen travellers' cheques, and Burroughs imagined him being apprehended with the words 'Are you Eric Trevor-Orme-Smith-Creighton also known as 'El Chinche' (The Bed Bug)?'[14]

Brian Howard, largely remembered as a model for Anthony Blanche in Evelyn Waugh's *Brideshead Revisited*, had also washed up in Tangier after a lifetime of failure and snobbery (questioned by the police in a wartime night-club, he had said his name was Brian Howard, and 'I live in Mayfair. No doubt *you* come from some dreary suburb.'[15]) In an unexpected literary conjunction he became a friend of Burroughs, whom he describes in a letter as 'a nice, if slightly long-winded, ex-Harvard creature of forty who is endeavouring to cure himself of morphinomania by taking this new medicine which the Germans invented during the war.'

> Unfortunately, the effects are so much stronger, and more delicious than morphine *itself* that he now spends his whole time running from chemist to chemist buying it – and spends all his money on it, too. I, myself, [have] experimented with it …

and really, it is quite *extraordinary*. . . . One loses all desire for alcohol (excellent, for me) and I walk around in a benign dream. . . . Here, it can be got without a prescription. . . . I cannot see that it can be physically harmful, in any way. And since, at the same time, it is quite heavenly – I think it rather a find.[16]

Burroughs liked Howard, whom he found a great comfort as an audience: 'Brian really digs my routines'. Unfortunately, having introduced Howard to dolophine, Burroughs found he had created a monster when Howard became addicted and proceeded to 'burn down' (make suspicious and unusable) every drugstore in town.[17]

Burroughs's own addiction was grim. He was injecting every two hours, and found the weaker Eukodol more compulsive than morphine, like a hot bath that wasn't quite hot enough: morphine had a point of satiation, like eating, but Eukodol was more like scratching an itch. He could now put a needle straight into his vein through a festering, gaping sore that stayed open like an obscene little mouth.[18]

Inevitably he wasn't getting much writing done, although he could feel a work of some sort taking shape. It was shaping up largely in letters to Ginsberg ('Maybe the real novel is letters to you', he wrote in June 1954) and some of Burroughs's funniest inventions never made it into the book, like leper chic:

Two elegant pansies in excruciatingly chic apartment [. . .]
P.1 (Bursting into the room) 'My dear, you'll never guess what I've got . . . Lab reports just in . . . Leprosy!'
P.2 'How Mediaeval of you!'
P.1 'I'm having a cloak designed by Antoine. Absolutely authentic. And I shall carry a bell . . .'[19]

The whole concept of the routine was taking on a further life of its own, and Burroughs attempted to define it. It wasn't merely symbolic or representational, but was 'subject to shlup over into "real" action at any time (like cutting off finger joint and so forth). In a sense the whole Nazi movement was a great, humourless, evil *routine* on Hitler's part.'[20]

In February 1955 he enclosed his 'Talking Asshole' routine in a letter to Ginsberg, later to figure in *Naked Lunch*. Having chewed its way out through its owner's trousers, it would then 'start talking on the street, shouting out that it wanted equal rights. It would get drunk too, and have crying jags, [saying] nobody loved it', until finally it takes over completely. Burroughs marvelled at the grotesqueness of his own work: it was almost like 'automatic writing' done by a hostile, independent entity that seemed to be saying, 'I will write what I please.'[21]

On a more conventional level, the nascent work had 'themes'. It was about the menace to the human spirit of scientific and author-itarian control, and something even more sinister behind that:

> Control, bureaucracy, regimentation, these are merely symptoms of a deeper sickness that no political or economic program can touch. What is the sickness itself?[22]

Burroughs didn't know, but for now he was cooking up a thriller-style scenario where evil scientists had devised an anti-dreaming drug that could remove the whole vital resource of inner freedom and subjectivity, and the region of intuition and symbolization where mythology and art were created.[23] With this dimension excised, people would become like interchangeable cogs in a machine. Burroughs's protagonist persona and his fictional comrades were engaged in a counter-conspiracy, trying to destroy the formula, and in one scenario the Burroughs figure is to be arrested and taken away by two policemen for use as a guinea pig in experiments. He shoots them both dead, the germ of the 'Hauser and O'Brien' section of *Naked Lunch*.

Burroughs aired these ideas to Ginsberg in letters and they reached fictional form in 'The Conspiracy', eventually published as a part of *Interzone*. On the run in New York after killing Hauser and O'Brien, the protagonist hides out with a reliable woman friend called Mary, near Columbia University. He tells her, as he has before, about the sense he sometimes has of train whistles, burning leaves, and piano music down a city street. His point is that this delicate and fleeting experience can be reliably reproduced by certain metabolic factors. Conversely, he says, scientists have now perfected the anti-dream drug, so it is now possible

to eliminate nostalgia, to occlude the whole dreaming, symbolizing faculty . . . the source of resistance, contact with the myth that gives each man the ability to live alone and unites him with all other life, is cut off. He becomes an automaton, an interchangeable quantity in the political and economic equation.[24]

It was a lifelong concern. In *The Place of Dead Roads*, written 30 years later, the young Burroughs figure, Kim, knows that dreams are 'a vital link to our biologic and spiritual destiny in space. Deprived of this air line we die.' It is set in the Wild West era, and Kim further knows that 'The way to kill a man or a nation is to cut off his dreams', as the whites were doing to the Indians: 'killing their dreams, their magic, their familiar spirits.'[25]

For now, in the mid-1950s, if there was the fictional anti-dream drug there was also an antidote, an idealized good drug, and in 'The Conspiracy' Burroughs still gave this role to yageine or telepathine.

Addiction to Eukodol was meanwhile making it almost impossible to work. Kiki had nursed him through one withdrawal, and he had tried paying Eric Gifford to dole out his supply in moderation and even keep his clothes (in the event Burroughs stole another lodger's clothing and escaped to the drugstore).

On another occasion he injected himself with hyoscine to eke out his dolophine, but he reacted badly and was found naked in the hallway in the middle of the night, sitting on a lavatory seat which he had wrenched off its moorings and singing 'Deep in the Heart of Texas'.

It wasn't funny at the time, but it reads like light relief compared to the depths of his drug habit, recorded in the 'Testimony Concerning A Sickness' appendix to *Naked Lunch*. He had left Dutch Tony's and moved to a room in the Casbah, the native quarter. Burroughs could now spend eight hours looking at his shoe, periodically sticking a needle into his grey fibrous flesh. He never washed or changed his clothes, and his trousers were shiny with grime. People rarely visited, and if they did he was indifferent to them drifting in and out of his field of vision. Had they died, he says, he would have simply waited to go through their pockets.

Burroughs had heard there was a new cure in London, and in spring 1956 he made a desperate break, taking an aeroplane flight with an eau de cologne bottle of junk solution. He was headed for Dr John Yerbury Dent, who gave him a new lease of life: '*Naked Lunch* would never have been written without Doctor Dent's treatment.'[26]

Dr Dent (1888–1962) had a small clinic at 34 Addison Road, on the corner with Holland Park Road (now redeveloped). Dent ('charcoal fire in the grate Scottish terrier cup of tea') explained the treatment, and Burroughs entered an associated nursing home on the Cromwell Road ('room with rose wall paper on the third floor').[27] Dent was the author of *Reactions of the Human Machine* (1936) and *Anxiety and its Treatment* (1941), honorary editor of the *British Journal of Addiction*, and a specialist in the treatment of alcoholics. His particular method involved a drug called apomorphine, which is prepared by boiling morphine in hydrochloric acid. It is non-euphoriant, induces severe vomiting, and was usually regarded as an emetic for use in aversion treatments, but Dent –

and Burroughs after him – thought it did far more; he thought it acted on the brain to regulate metabolism in such a way that the actual mechanism of addiction was removed.

Much of Dent's success must have been due to his character and personal care. Burroughs found the withdrawal an ordeal but he had nothing but praise for Dent: as he wrote to Ginsberg in May 1956, Dent was interested in yage and Mayan archaeology and when Burroughs couldn't sleep he would sit with him until five in the morning talking. Burroughs was cured in a week, and very impressed with his treatment: Paul Bowles noted a couple of years later that 'Bill B goes to London now solely to visit his beloved Dr Dent.'[28]

Burroughs also took up the abdominal exercise system of F. A. Hornibrook – author of the once best-selling book *The Culture of*

Dr John Yerbury Dent, pioneer of the apomorphine method for treating addiction. Burroughs said *Naked Lunch* would never have been written without Dent.

the Abdomen (1924) – whom Dent seems to have introduced him to personally (he saw personal pupils at his flat in Victoria). Burroughs didn't otherwise like London, which he found over-regulated and class-conscious. He stayed at 44 Egerton Gardens in Knightsbridge, and after his withdrawal he not only had horrible nightmares but was sexually propositioned by a half-senile Liberal peer and the writer Angus Wilson. As he wrote to Ginsberg, it was all 'Too horrid.'[29]

Leaving London that summer, Burroughs went to stay with Alan Ansen in Venice. He was feeling better than he had for years and had taken up rowing, but he still tended to drink too much when he was off junk, and disgraced himself at Peggy Guggenheim's palazzo. She was throwing a cocktail party for the British consul, with her flunkies and modern artworks everywhere, and Burroughs was advised it was the custom to kiss her hand. 'I will be glad to kiss her cunt if that is the custom', he said,[30] and rapidly found himself as socially welcome as the boy he had been in St Louis.

That August he wrote a long letter to Dr Dent, later published in *The British Journal of Addiction* and *Naked Lunch* as 'Letter From A Master Addict' – a strange conflation of active and passive – 'to Dangerous Drugs'. His general health was excellent, he said, and he now had no desire to use any drug. He sent his regards to Hornibrook, saying he used his exercises with excellent results, and then reviewed his entire drug-taking career including opiates, yage, cannabis, cocaine, Benzedrine and barbiturates, strongly endorsing apomorphine as the way out of addiction.

Burroughs went back to Tangier via Tripoli and Algiers, which was swept with terror attacks against the French. He ate lunch in a milk bar ('small place with mirrors on the walls, square pillars covered with mirrors, great jars full of fruit juice, salads, ice cream . . .'[31]), which was bombed shortly afterwards with horrifying carnage. It later resonated in Burroughs's mind with Graham Greene's description of a milk bar bombing in Vietnam.

Back in Tangier, Burroughs settled into the Hotel Villa Muniria at 1 calle Magallanes. He described it as 'the original anything goes joint', and it was run by two retired prostitutes from colonial Saigon, who were themselves opiate users.[32] He was off drugs but still known to some of the local Spanish-speaking boys as *El Hombre Invisible*, the Invisible Man. Like Bill Gains, he seemed to have mastered a grey, ghostly anonymity, as if his trademark hat, coat and glasses were quietly walking around the town on their own.

Someone who did notice him was Colonel Gerald Richardson, Tangier's British police chief. Burroughs built himself another orgone box at the Muniria, and Richardson writes of an educated American drug addict, living on money from home, whom he calls Morphine Minnie:

> Morphine Minnie certainly got up to some strange tricks. He had a large box specially made for him with holes punched in the sides: in appearance it was like a long cabin trunk. On occasions he would induce a young boy to enter the box and lie down in it – fully clothed, I hasten to add – and he would put the lid back on. After he judged the boy had been in there long enough he would open the box again, let the boy out and send him on his way. He would then get into the box himself, and lie down. When he later emerged, so far as I was able to understand it – and he was a strenuous advocate for the practice – he was supposed to be rejuvenated.[33]

Richardson might not have understood what was going on, but Burroughs was certainly rejuvenated, largely because he was off junk. He wrote to tell Ginsberg of the pleasure he got just from walking, or rowing a boat, and that he had even had a spontaneous orgasm while doing his Hornibrook exercises.[34] This was rare, Burroughs said; the only spontaneous waking orgasm of this sort that he'd had before had been while he was back in Texas, inside his orgone box.

Kerouac came to visit early in 1957 and was astonished at Burroughs's new vitality. Burroughs was now settled into the most important bout of writing in his life, producing the material that would later be extracted into *Naked Lunch*, along with *The Soft Machine* and *The Ticket That Exploded*. Kerouac helped him with some typing, but he found the material nightmarish. What was going on with this stuff? 'Don't ask me', Burroughs said,

> I get these messages from other planets – I'm apparently some kind of agent from another planet but I haven't got my orders clearly decoded yet.
> [. . .]
> I'm shitting out my educated Middlewest background for once and for all. It's a matter of catharsis, where I say the most horrible thing I can think of.[35]

This was particularly true of a text called 'Word', composed around this time, which marks the transition to a *Naked Lunch*-type writing (only a few fragments made it into the final selection of *Lunch* but the whole 'Word' text is, if anything, more grotesque and extreme). The work in progress seemed to be having an alarming effect on its author's personality, inasmuch as he still had one: 'Whenever he talked, it was through so many layers of impersonation – British lord doing spluttering mad scientist doing Mr Hyde, and so forth, – that Jack couldn't discern a trace of any real man he had once known.'[36]

Burroughs had now got to know Paul Bowles better, describing him along with Dr Dent as one of two 'really great people' he'd come to know since moving to Tangier ('telepathy flows like water'),[37] and Bowles has described Burroughs as he was at this time. He was living in a single ground-floor room at the Muniria, with its door opening straight on to the garden, and one wall of the room was pockmarked with bullet holes. Another wall was covered in photographs Burroughs had taken, mostly on his Amazon travels. Bowles liked to hear him talk about these trips, and Burroughs told him about yage, the point of it being 'the facilitation of mental telepathy and emotional empathy'.[38] Burroughs said he'd communicated with the Indians on yage, even though he couldn't speak their language.

Burroughs was now consuming plenty of his home-made cannabis fudge or *majoun* (of which he was very proud; he cooked it up on a little stove and ate it every day, offering it to anyone who was interested) as well as smoking kif cigarettes: he would pace around the room talking and picking up joints that were simultaneously alight in two or three ashtrays. The chaotic manuscripts of what would become *Naked Lunch* were piling up under his desk, getting trodden on and covered in rat droppings. He would pick up sheets at random and read them to Bowles, laughing 'a good deal, as well he might, since it is very funny, but from reading he would suddenly (the paper still in hand) go into a bitter conversational attack upon whatever aspect of life had prompted the passage he had just read'.[39]

Burroughs found his routines would come so fast he could hardly write them down; they shook him 'like a great black wind through the bones' (the phrase is from Saint-John Perse, as Oliver Harris has noted[40]) and he would have laughing fits that were heard by the man next door. He sent routines and chunks of work in progress (currently called Interzone) to Ginsberg, along with rationales of what he intended to do in his novel, which he found clarified it.

The real theme, he wrote, was the desecration of the 'Human Image' by control addicts; addiction and control were the central evils, and the addiction was spread as a virus. At times, he said, he felt like a Bosch or Dante. By October 1957 he felt it was about lost innocence and the Fall, with some form of redemption possible through 'knowledge of basic life processes'.[41]

A decision to set the book largely in Tangier was a breakthrough, and more of it fell into place with a visit to Denmark in 1957 (at the invitation of Kells Elvins, who was now married to a Danish film star and living in Copenhagen). Scandinavia seemed hideously clean and dead to Burroughs, like the jazz that flourished there, and it became 'Freelandt' in the work in progress, where places figured as ways of life and states of mind. The action occurred in 'a super-imposed place', Burroughs explained to Ginsberg, which was at once South America, the States, Tangier and Scandinavia. Characters wandered around, so that a Turkish bath in Sweden might suddenly open into the South American jungle: 'the shift from schizophrenia to addiction takes a character from one *place* to another.' [Burroughs's emphasis][42]

Naked Lunch is famously obscene but often weirdly beautiful: 'Motel . . . Motel . . . Motel . . . broken neon arabesque . . . loneliness moans across the continent like fog horns over still oily water of tidal rivers . . .'.[43] It is also one of the century's funniest works: 'Now that [S. J.] Perelman is dead, Bill is our foremost humorist', as Paul Bowles later wrote.[44] A 'battalion of rampant bores' prowls the streets looking for victims, including an old explorer, an English colonial, and a literary avant-gardist ('Of course the only writing worth considering now is to be found in scientific reports . . .'). The explorer catches his prey in a grand, empty, 1890 style hotel lobby and paralyses him with a curare blow dart, administering artificial respiration with his foot while talking at length about his misadventures in the Upper Baboonasshole (a reliable location in Burroughs's comic topography and apparently based on a place he'd actually been to in the Amazon, Upper Babunasa).[45]

The world's religions also become the subject of a blasphemous routine catching the self-interested nature of Islam, with the Mecca Chamber of Commerce; the miracle workings of Christ (seen as fakir-type tricks of a kind positively disdained by Buddhism); and the self-contained nature of Buddha, who tires of waiting for the

Man and decides to metabolize his own junk. Central to the book are various threats to the autonomy and authenticity of the individual – in danger of being telepathically controlled by Senders, swamped by self-replicating Divisionists cloning themselves, or absorbed by Liquefactionists – and these are opposed by the Factualists, chief among them Burroughs himself, the straight-shooting Korzybskian.

Inevitably, being Burroughs, the idea of inauthenticity and negativity involves some savage joking about queer posturing – he had written to Ginsberg that 'swish fairies' ought to be killed, not even as traitors to queerness, but 'for selling out the human race to the forces of negation and death'[46] – but it has larger resonances. Dr Benway's ruthless manipulation of the psyche is entirely topical in the era of lobotomies (another of Burroughs's mad doctors is 'Fingers Schafer, The Lobotomy Kid'), electric brain implants, conditioning and Behaviourism.

Naked Lunch is also notorious for its hanging sequences, which have been explained not entirely convincingly as a Swiftian satire on capital punishment. Hanging and its sexual side effects were

Burroughs pretends to hang Alan Ansen; photo by Ginsberg, Villa Muniria, 1957.

a lifelong preoccupation of Burroughs, and it is more likely that this was something he heard of in childhood that stayed with him as a sexual fixation.

This repetitive nature of fixation and fantasy is expressed in Burroughs's idea that what excites people sexually is a movie, but even if his fascination with hanging has a personal basis it is no less thematic within the concerns of his work, representing among other things the involuntary nature of sexual excitation. Burroughs wasn't entirely comfortable with sexuality and life in the body, and he had a half-squeamish, half-prurient fascination with a pain/pleasure nexus that was, perhaps, ultimately ascetic. At one point a character is, in a suggestive phrase, 'hanged, convict [*sic*] of the guilty possession of a nervous system'.[47]

The same sensibility can be seen all through Burroughs's writing: in *Lunch*, Johnny anoints Mary with gasoline from a Chimu jar and they copulate under a great magnifying glass set in the roof before bursting into flames; the addicts of the Black Meat eat and vomit and eat compulsively to the point of exhaustion; and in a letter routine Burroughs imagines Paul Bowles compulsively ecstatic over a huge female centipede, which he rips apart and rubs on himself: his body jerks in uncontrollable spasms as a current runs up his spine, 'a penetration unspeakably vile and delicious, to burst in his brain like a white hot, searing, rocket.'[48] Eukodol made him imagine an even stronger quintessence of junk called Super Plus Square Root H: once addicted, without it 'you die in convulsions of over-sensitivity, flashes of pleasure intensify to acute agony in a fraction of a second'.[49]

There was sad news when Burroughs returned to Tangier from Denmark. Kiki, one of the relatively few people with whom he had managed a simple and uncomplicated but affectionate sexual relationship, was dead. When Burroughs had gone to Britain for the apomorphine cure, Kiki had taken up with a Cuban bandleader. In September 1957, in Madrid, the man found Kiki with a girl and stabbed him to death in a fit of jealousy. As Barry Miles has suggested, Burroughs may have felt personal regret for the circumstances that left Kiki to the Cuban; at any event, he dreamed about him repeatedly and often sadly over the next four decades.

After Kerouac, more friends came to visit Burroughs in his last couple of years in Tangier, the era of his great writing jag. Alan Ansen came and so did Ginsberg, for whom Burroughs still had strong feelings: during Kerouac's visit he had cried when talking about him. Unfortunately Ginsberg came to stay with his new partner, Peter Orlovsky, whom Burroughs disliked.

Burroughs's friends helped with editing the chaos of paper that became *Naked Lunch*, the messiness of the manuscript concordant with its collage aesthetic. Burroughs's description of it is entirely characteristic and has something bereft about it, despite the crazed energy of the text, with the selected chapters forming a kind of collage or mosaic 'with the cryptic significance of juxtaposition, like objects abandoned in a hotel drawer . . .'.[50]

The manuscript went through various titles, including Interzone (from Tangier), Word Hoard (from Anglo-Saxon poetry), Ignorant Armies (from the ignorant armies that clash by night in Matthew Arnold's poem 'Dover Beach'), and finally *Naked Lunch*; the suggestion was Kerouac's, from Ginsberg's fortuitous misreading of 'naked lust' but soon taking on an intense appropriateness: Ginsberg's phrase in a poem, 'reality sandwiches', is a paraphrase, and already in the dedication of *Howl* (1956) Ginsberg could write of Burroughs as the author of *Naked Lunch*, an endless novel that would drive everyone mad.

Perhaps cathartic, the great writing jag precipitated or at least coincided with the kind of feelings and changes Burroughs more usually felt from being in analysis (he had no analyst in Tangier, although he was interested in the self-analysis system of Karen Horney and may have been using it; this was, in effect, a process of completely unflinching introspection). He felt a shift in his sexual orientation around late 1957, with a buried and betrayed heterosexual youth trapped inside him, all but murdered. He was never supposed to be queer at all, he wrote to Ginsberg, and now the 'whole original trauma' was out; it had been such a horror he was afraid his heart would stop, and had developed psycho-somatic problems. These feelings continued for some time. Sometimes it was boys, sometimes it was girls, and sometimes he didn't know if he was interested in men, women, both, or neither. 'I think neither. Just can't dig the natives on this planet.'[51]

Burroughs was already fascinated by the idea of viruses, and he was disturbed to read that they were the only life forms that reacted favourably to atomic radiation: suddenly he visualized centipedes a hundred feet long being eaten by viruses the size of bed bugs under a grey sky of atomic fall-out.[52] In January 1958 *Time* magazine ran an article about a mystery virus outbreak at a US Air Force base in Oklahoma, and Burroughs connected this with an illness that seemed to be going around Tangier: he had to get out for his health, he wrote to Ginsberg. The place was 'plague ridden' with 'some obscure virus'.[53]

Ginsberg was in Paris, with Orlovsky, and in January 1958 Burroughs took a plane and followed them there.

7

Paris: Cut-ups at the Beat Hotel

Allen Ginsberg and Peter Orlovsky had been staying in a cheap
hotel at 9 rue Gît-le-Coeur – a quiet, lane-like old street in the Left
Bank's Latin Quarter, running towards the Seine and the Ile de la
Cité. Rooms were hard to get, but Ginsberg managed to reserve
one for Burroughs by renting it well ahead of his arrival, and in
mid-January 1958 Burroughs took up residence in a basic room
at $25 a month.[1]

Ginsberg was apprehensive about the emotional claims
Burroughs might make on him, remembering his 'schlupping'
intensity during their relationship in New York, but he needn't have
worried. Burroughs was in an unusually good state of mind, and
although they had sex together he explained that he hadn't come to
hit on Allen but to complete his analysis, 'to clear up psychoanalytic
blocks left etc.'[2] Burroughs had been analysing himself introspec-
tively, meditating every afternoon; in the words of Barry Miles, he
'accepted all the unpleasant or horrible fantasies that entered his
head as a real part of himself, and instead of suppressing them with
a shudder of revulsion, he concentrated on each one, developing
and analysing it in more or less the same manner as he developed
ideas to their absolute limits in his routines'.[3]

Burroughs felt there was something terrible in his infancy –
something about his nurse, perhaps – and he couldn't quite uncover it on his own. The analyst he chose was Marc Schlumberger.
Around fifteen years older than Burroughs, Schlumberger was the

son of Jean Schlumberger, founder of the *Nouvelle Revue Française,* and one of his own problems was that he found it difficult to come to terms with having a homosexual father. At the time he analysed Burroughs he was President of the Paris Psychoanalytic Society, the SPP, and highly respected. Burroughs saw him twice a week at ten dollars a session.

Burroughs's psychic travails in Tangier had also brought him an uncharacteristically benevolent vision of something peaceful at the centre of existence, like a central well of love; this was very much on Ginsberg's wavelength, since Ginsberg had already seen what he called 'a benevolent sentient centre to the whole Creation'; a 'big peaceful Lovebrain'.[4]

Burroughs had been safely off Eukodol since seeing Dr Dent, but one of the peculiarities of Paris until recently was the paregoric-style availability of codeine preparations over the counter at every pharmacy, in the form of syrup or packets of sugar-coated pills. A recent memoir of Paris has a minor English poet, lodging above Shakespeare and Co. bookshop, rummaging agitatedly under his bed until he finds a little brown bottle, taking a long swig, and then relaxing with the words 'Captain Cody's Midnight Rangers to the rescue . . .'.[5] There have been a number of theories about the legal status of these preparations, one of them being that the French authorities wanted to provide a 'soft fix' for the French colonials who developed a taste for opium in French Indo-China.

Whatever the reason, Burroughs found this state of affairs very congenial. A couple of decades later, in a short text entitled 'Paris Please Stay the Same', he relates that when he heard codethyline was now available only on prescription

I felt the same deep pang of loss as I experienced when they ripped the urinals from the streets, tore down Les Halles, and cut down the trees in the Grand Socco of Tangier [. . .] 'Tis gone,

'Tis gone . . . another corner of the 19th century . . . brightness
falls from the air . . . the urinals, Les Halles, the trees . . .
'Codethyline Houdé . . .'
'Oui Monsieur . . . une ou deux?'
'Deux'
I'll remember her that way.[6]

Burroughs remembered going to bed with the flu, a pile of science
fiction books on his bedside table and some Codethyline Houdé;
soon he was 'squirming with sheer comfort beneath the covers like
some 18th-century English gentleman who has taken to his bed for
the winter.'[7]

By February 1958 Burroughs already had a light habit again, to
Ginsberg's concern, but he assured him in a letter – Ginsberg was
briefly visiting England – that it was nothing to be alarmed about,
and that he was even hoping to use it experimentally in his analysis.[8]

Burroughs was comfortable at the nameless hotel on the rue
Gît-le-Coeur, which became known as the Beat Hotel; in due course
Ginsberg, Burroughs, Gregory Corso and Brion Gysin all lived
there. 'It was just a very nice place,' said Burroughs later, 'old old
old. Middle ages. And Madame Rachou was very nice.'[9] Madame
Rachou was a short and formidable French woman who kept the
place under her very watchful eye, and she liked Burroughs. No
doubt she approved of his good manners and conservative clothing,
but she liked artistic types in general; she always remembered that
when she worked in a cafe as a girl she had served Monet.

There were thirteen categories of hotel in Paris, and the Beat
Hotel was category thirteen. The sanitation was primitive, and hot
water and electricity were not to be taken liberties with: a bath
could only be had by prior arrangement, and Madame Rachou
could tell from her central electricity switchboard if anyone was
using more than their forty-watt bulb, which would bring her
knocking on the door. But wine was cheap in the downstairs bar,

Madame Rachou was really quite tolerant in her way, and the place has now entered the mythology, with the usual *Rashomon*-style effects. In the words of Burroughs:

'Madame Rachou was very mysterious and arbitrary about whom she would let into her hotel. 'She has her orders,' Brion Gysin always said.'

Or as Brion Gysin remembered it,

'William Burroughs always used to say sententiously: 'Madame Rachou has her orders.' Whatever did he mean?' [1C]

Burroughs's friendship with Gysin was still in the future, and for now he remained on best friend terms with Ginsberg. In June 1958 they went with Gregory Corso to a Paris party in honour of Man Ray and Marcel Duchamp. Ginsberg was a fan of Duchamp's and became excited, crawling around after Duchamp on all fours and calling him *cher maître*. Ginsberg asked Duchamp to kiss Burroughs ('a symbolic passing of the mantle from the great French surrealist to his contemporary American successor', says Ted Morgan[11]) and Duchamp went along with it in good humour, giving Burroughs a peck on the forehead.

The following month Ginsberg and Burroughs set off on a pilgrimage for a less sunny meeting with Louis-Ferdinand Céline, still a controversial figure after siding with the Germans in the War. Highly regarded by Samuel Beckett and Henry Miller, Céline was also esteemed by the Beats after Burroughs introduced them to his work in the 1940s. 'It seemed to me that Céline was actually the most compassionate French writer of his time', Kerouac wrote later; 'a writer of great, supremely great charm and intelligence and no one compares to him'. For Kerouac he had 'that modern flamboyant tone of knocking the chip off the shoulder of horror, that sincere agony, that redeeming shrug and laugh.'[12] It was from Céline and his 'style telegraphique' . . . using ellipsis to capture a spoken effect . . . that Burroughs and the Beats took their free use of dots.

Céline had been a doctor, practising among the poor and sometimes refusing his fee, and he was still just practising when Ginsberg and Burroughs found him living in the rundown Seine suburb of Meudon ('shabby villas with flaking stucco'; it reminded Burroughs of the outskirts of Los Angeles). They could tell they were approaching *chez* Céline from the sound of dogs barking: big dogs that he kept, as he explained to Burroughs and Ginsberg, 'because of the *Jeeews*.'

Life was full of disagreeable surprises, Céline said, and then there were other, more paranoid aggravations: the druggist wouldn't fill his prescriptions, and the postmaster was destroying his post ('We walked right into a Céline novel'). Ginsberg asked him about contemporary writers – Beckett, Sartre, Simone de Beauvoir, everyone he could think of – and Céline casually dismissed them all, one after another: 'Every year there is a new fish in the literary pond.'

Ginsberg presented Céline with some books, including Burroughs's *Junky* – what an association copy that would be, if it hadn't almost certainly been binned – some poems by Corso, and his own *Howl*. Céline clearly had no intention of wasting his time and glanced at them without much interest before laying them aside, as Burroughs remembered it, 'sort of definitively'.[13]

Céline waved them a cordial goodbye as they left. They had met a legendary figure, and they knew it; one of the true greats of the twentieth century. Burroughs had recently met another truly great writer, or so he thought, in the person of Jacques Stern. Burroughs had become friendly with Gregory Corso (who picked up a junk habit in consequence, although Burroughs had warned him it was evil stuff). A survivor of the juvenile reformatory system, Corso was probably the least intellectual and most extrovert of the Beats, and he had heard about Stern as a millionaire French junky intellectual, crippled by polio, who hung out in the cafes of the Latin Quarter. Peering into a Bentley one day in spring 1958, and seeing a crippled man inside, he realized it was him and thought he should meet Burroughs.

Corso carried him – he didn't weigh very much – up the stairs to Burroughs's room at the Beat Hotel, and they got along splendidly. Burroughs felt Stern was the most interesting person he had met in Paris. They were both Harvard graduates and both steeped in drugs, and Stern was additionally a gourmet, bon viveur and collector of first editions, with a serious collection of Molière. He also had a beautiful wife whom Burroughs took to, Dini (she was a 'really nice person', Burroughs reported to Ginsberg, telling him how much he liked her).[14]

Burroughs and Stern went to London together in October 1958 where they took Dent's cure again, renting a flat at 2 Mansfield Street. Burroughs hadn't yet realised that Stern was an incorrigible liar and fantasist, spinning stories of a yacht, a terrible crash in his Bentley, a previous and completely fictitious visit to Dr Dent, the personal invention of a new method of psychotherapy (called 'functional therapy', this had allegedly cured four long-term 'psycho cases' he had encountered at Dr Dent's, and considerably interested Burroughs) and the forthcoming publication of his novel *Fluke*.

Stern said *Fluke* was coming out from the august British publishing firm of Faber & Faber, but this was another fantasy. In the event Stern self-published it into overnight obscurity, but Burroughs was blown away by the extracts he was shown. It was great, he told Ginsberg, really great, 'not jive talk great'. He thought Stern's writing was far better than his own, or Kerouac's, or Ginsberg's; he was the greatest writer of their time.[15] Fragments of Stern, otherwise unseen, survive in Burroughs's cut-up work, notably *The Soft Machine*.

The impression that Jacques Stern made on Burroughs reveals an oddly gullible and easily enthused side to the seasoned voyager and hardened experimental pragmatist that Burroughs might otherwise seem to be, on his worldly-wise mission to 'wise up the marks'. But this was hardly more than a rehearsal for one of the key meetings of his life, when he fell under the influence of the unfailingly poised and regally smooth artist Brion Gysin, whom he would later describe as 'the only man I have ever respected'.[16] Paul Bowles had a less positive view of Gysin, saying 'Anyone who came in contact with Brion fell ten years behind in his career.'[17]

Gysin had been born in England in 1916, son of a Swiss father and a Canadian mother. After his father was killed during the First War, he was brought up by his mother in Canada and then sent to the Catholic boarding school of Downside. He became an artist in Europe, on the fringes of the surrealist group, but André Breton took a dislike to his work and had it removed from a group show in 1935. Unlike Burroughs, Gysin was interested in worldly success of a very European kind – Chevalier of this, Order of that, Academy of the other – and he became embittered by his failure to find it, which increased his belief that the art world was a conspiracy. Most of the world's troubles, in fact, were due to Jews and women.

Gysin was a partisan for black and Arab culture, and Islamic script was an influence on his work. His two most famous projects, the cut-up method and the Dream Machine, were still slightly in the future, and at this time his art tended to two or three distinct 'lines.' One was abstract calligraphy, combining a fascination with Arabic with his experience of learning Japanese (with the us Army, although the war was over before he could use it). Gysin's calligraphy resembles that of the American artist Mark Tobey, who was interested in Eastern culture and Zen, but within a Parisian context it aligns him more closely with the Lettrist movement, as he knew. Before being taken over and transformed by Guy Debord, who re-made them into the Situationists, the Lettrists were led by Isidore Isou, who wanted to break verbal art down to individual letters (and cinema down to simple, non-representational alternations of darkness and white light). Much Lettrist work consisted of graphic scripts and alphabets, midway between hieroglypics, shorthand and old books of magic.

Another of Gysin's art lines consisted of dabbed and spattered ink dashes, like the work of Henri Michaux, in which figures and events could be seen: there were crowds, battles, dancers milling around a desert fire and more, all in the eye of the beholder. Gysin had a remarkable flair for these, lying ultimately – like the things that can be seen in firelight or marble – within a Salvador Dalí-style 'paranoia-critical' aesthetic, and they fascinated Burroughs.

Dalí was in the habit of looking at newsprint upside down: 'Instead of reading the news, I look at it and I see it. Even as an adolescent, I saw, among the typographical spirals, and just by squinting, soccer games as they would look on television. It even happened that before half time, I had to go and rest, so exhausted was I by the ups and downs of the game.'[18] Looking at Gysin's work, Burroughs had to gaze at it until something caught, and suddenly he was 'in':

> Usually I get in by a port of entry, as I call it. It is often a face through whose eyes the picture opens into a landscape and I go literally right through that eye into that landscape. Sometimes it is rather like an archway . . . little details or a special spot of colours makes the port of entry and then the entire picture will suddenly become a three-dimensional frieze in plaster or jade or some other precious material . . . Now you suddenly see all sorts of things there. Beautiful jungle landscape . . . All sorts of faces . . . monkey faces . . . typical withered monkey faces. Very archetypical in this world.[19]

Burroughs and Gysin had been wary and disdainful of each other in Tangier – Burroughs found Gysin too smooth, and Gysin despised Burroughs for narcotics, further disregarding him as too Spanish (i.e. hanging out with Spanish rather than Arab boys) – but Paul Bowles had assured Gysin that if only he would get to know Burroughs then he would like him.

Gysin had a wonderfully mythomaniac 'memory' of seeing Burroughs in Tangier back in 1954, when Burroughs had come into an exhibition of pictures by Gysin's young Arab friend Hamri. It was at the Rembrandt Hotel and Burroughs had wheeled in, 'arms and legs flailing, talking a mile a minute',

> . . . he trailed long vines of Bannisteria caapi from the Upper Amazon after him and old Mexican bullfight posters fluttered out from under his long trench coat instead of a shirt. An odd blue light often flashed around under the brim of his hat.[20]

And now they met again in Paris in the Autumn of 1958, on the Place St Michel. Burroughs was in a hurry, rushing to his analytic session, but he invited Gysin to drop round for tea at his room in the Beat Hotel, number 15.

In due course Gysin moved into the hotel, where Burroughs saw he was doing 'GREAT painting', and, like the work of Stern, it was 'great in the old sense, not jive talk great'. Gysin, said Burroughs, was doing in his painting what Burroughs was doing himself, opening up real psychic spaces. Gysin's painting was a hole in 'so-called "reality"' through which he could explore 'an actual place existing in outer space'. Gysin himself had a beautiful Chinese story about the master painter who bowed three times, stepped into his painting and disappeared.[21]

Burroughs felt Gysin understood everything he had ever tried to do, and Gysin largely replaced Ginsberg in his affections, but this time without any sexual relationship. Ginsberg considered

Gysin unhealthily superstitious when he eventually met him, and meanwhile wondered at the new slants manifesting themselves in Burroughs's letters.

Gysin had encountered magic in Morocco ('Magic calls itself The Other Method for controlling matter and knowing space. In Morocco, magic is practiced more assiduously than hygiene'[22]). He thought of compiling a grimoire of North African spells, and he believed he had lost his restaurant, the 1001 Nights, through magical machinations: he had found a package hidden in a ventilator shaft, including seven shards of broken mirror, seven pebbles, seven seeds, and hair, blood and gum, together with an inscription to the Djinn of the Hearth or the Smoke, 'May Massa Brahim [Brion] leave this house as the smoke leaves the fire' – by the ventilation shaft – 'never to return'.[23] There had already been some attempt to poison Gysin, it seemed, but this did it. Gysin quarrelled with his backer, a rich woman – or, as he told it sometimes, he put his signature to something and the woman swindled him out of the business, or he was swindled by a pair of early Scientologists – and he was gone.

Typical of Gysin's magical spiels was his talking to a friend and admirer of his work, Terry Wilson, about the Little People; 'I can show you lots right here in this pad', he said. In his book *Here to Go* Wilson discreetly notes that he couldn't conceive of these things – whatever they were – as beings. In fact they were the patterns of wood grain on a door, which Wilson could see as living but not actually sentient.[24]

Burroughs had always been a believer in the irrational and occult. There had been his nannies; his visions; a belief in life after death (which he'd argued about with his rationalist father); adolescent curses; Harvard-era reading about Tibetan Magic and the mainstream Western magic of Eliphas Levi; his passion for telepathy; his sense of the self as a haunted site of visitations and controlling, competing powers; and perhaps above all, growing stronger as he grew older, his sense of a 'magical universe' where nothing happens by accident. In the authorized words of Ted Morgan, checked by Burroughs, this sense that behind ordinary reality was a reality of spirits, curses, possession and phantoms was 'the single most important element of his life'.[25]

Gysin consolidated this side of Burroughs in a super-surreal conflation of reality and dream, and soon Burroughs was reporting to Ginsberg that nothing could stop the power of a 'real dream'. He meant this literally, he added. He could dream money into his pocket, and he could dream up heroin and opium: the previous morning he'd woken up junk sick and out of money, dreamed of opium, and then a friend had come in and given him a piece. Of course, he said,

> life is literally a dream, or rather the projection of a dream. That is why political action fails . . . But the whole exist-ing system can be dreamed away if we get enough people dreaming on the Gysin level.[26]

Gysin had a particularly enthralling spiel about Hassan I Sabbah, the Old Man of the Mountains, an eleventh-century Persian who ruled a network of spies and assassins from his stronghold at Alamut. It is said he inspired his followers with drug-induced visions of paradise, and that we get the words 'hashishin' and 'assassin' from him. Most of this is apocryphal, as is the quotation attributed to him – which would become important to Burroughs in the 1960s – 'Nothing is true, everything is permitted.'

Burroughs's analysis had meanwhile come to a head in Paris, where by July 1958 he came to believe he had witnessed a miscar-riage by Mary, 'the evil governess', and that the foetus had been burned in a furnace in his presence; that was the 'murder' lurking in his background.[27] With the climaxes that his analysis had been reaching, he already seemed to have gone through ten years' worth of changes in the year he had been at the Beat Hotel. And now, with 1959 coming up, he was going to live through probably the strangest single year of his life, and one of the most important.

Along with Stern and Gysin, Burroughs had met some younger Americans in Paris, notably a Texan named Mack Shell Thomas ('Shell' to Burroughs) who played the saxophone. He taught Burroughs a method for getting rid of unwelcome visitors; he was to look at them while silently thinking to himself 'I hate you – I love you – I hate you – I love you – I hate you – I love you . . .'. No doubt the combination of apparent attention and inward distractedness did make visitors uncomfortable, but for those who failed to receive the broadcast properly there was a further technique of simply visualizing them – their image-spirits, as it were – outside the room, in the hope that their bodies would follow.

Burroughs had great hopes from Shell, Gysin and Stern – 'three mystics I had hoped to form nucleus and get something definite and usable'[28]– but they foundered. His relationship with Stern cooled, and in spring 1959, at the height of American anti-drug, anti-Beatnik hysteria, Shell had gone back to Texas where he was not only in possession of heroin but, as if to advertise the fact, loudly dressed and carrying a saxophone. He got twenty years.[29]

Meanwhile, as Burroughs reported to Ginsberg in January 1959, paranormal occurrences were coming so thick and fast he could barely get them down on paper.[30] Gysin introduced him to the practice of mirror-gazing, for hours on end, until identity dissolved and strange things could be seen. Gysin saw nineteenth-century scientists in their laboratories, and journeys across steppes. This mirror-gazing could go on for 24 hours or more, with a friend passing the occasional joint round the door. Burroughs saw his own hands turn 'completely inhuman, thick, black-pink, with white tendrils growing out where the finger tips had been', and by the summer he saw himself turn into a creature with a face of black, boiling-looking fuzz.[31] And the most extraordinary thing, to Burroughs, was that other people seemed to be seeing these things, so it wasn't just illusion (the other people included, most notably, Stern and Gysin, as well as people who looked at him oddly in restaurants).

After Burroughs wrote the 'Fats Terminal' section of *Naked Lunch* – Terminal organizes a purple-assed baboon hunt from motorcyles, in the manner of pig-sticking, but we later meet him in far worse shape as a translucent, foetal monkey, with a round, lamprey disk-type mouth – Gysin showed him an amber bead from a magic Arab necklace, and in it Burroughs saw Terminal's face.

Things became even weirder after Burroughs bought a small, shiny stainless steel ball on a chain from one of Paris's many occult bookshops, la Table d'Emeraude (after the 'as above, so below' Emerald Tablet of Hermes Trismegistus) which was nearby at 21 rue de la Huchette, just on the other side of the Place Saint-Michel. This ball was probably meant as a dowsing ball, to be suspended by hand in order to see which way it swung or rotated (a practice used, at its most prosaic, for sexing chicken eggs) but Burroughs and Gysin used it instead for scrying, a technique akin to crystal ball gazing.

Scrying was used most famously by the Elizabethan magician Dr Dee and his assistant Kelley. They – or more particularly Kelley, who was something of a trickster – would look into an obsidian mirror, now in the British Museum, to see angelic spirits. Burroughs hung the ball on its chain in his room, and when Gysin came in he looked at it and saw Tangier, more specifically his old restaurant. Burroughs looked too, and together they saw a Moslem funeral carrying a body downstairs.

Burroughs noticed various phenomena in the following months: the ball seemed to be attracted towards a mirror, and at times Burroughs himself felt pushed away from the ball by a physical sensation he could barely describe, like a 'new dimension of gravity'.[32] He was spooked, and slept with the light on.

With or without the ball, he was having visions. In one there was an 'underwater medium, strange enclosed spheres moving through it.' He was in one of these spheres, watching 'Beautiful pink and black landscapes, people of black, flexible metal, people covered with green – brown – red – fuzz. Live, flying saucers like flat fish full of black fuzz.[33]

Burroughs wrote that in Tangier, where he went back for a short holiday in April 1959. There was a big anti-drugs crackdown in progress, which was to have unfortunate consequences. Burroughs's old acquaintance Paul Lund was taken in for questioning, and some incriminating correspondence from Burroughs was found. This concerned Burroughs's former and not very serious plan to import and sell Moroccan grass in Paris, but – particularly since it was coded, with some obfuscatory business about 'camel saddles' – it had caused Burroughs to be mistakenly implicated as the Paris contact of a hard drug ring.

It was a nuisance, but Burroughs's mind was now on other things. Death was not final, although a powerful lobby – a conspiracy almost, certainly a vested interest – tried to convince people it was, and he had discovered that there were literally billions of worlds. He was getting into dangerous areas, but he wouldn't turn back, even if he could: 'Let it come down – '.[34]

Burroughs was still writing *Naked Lunch*, and Allen Ginsberg was still trying to get it published. Gysin recalls Burroughs at work: bits of manuscript

floated around the hermetically sealed room as Burroughs, thrashing about in an ectoplasmic cloud of smoke, ranted through the gargantuan roles of Doc Benway, A.J., Clem and Jody, and hundreds of others he never had time to ram through the typewriter.[35]

Ginsberg had already, in 1957, taken some *Lunch* manuscript to the Paris-based erotica publisher Maurice Girodias, who did a thriving trade in English language 'DBs', or Dirty Books, under his

Olympia Press imprint. Along with pseudonymous potboilers like *There's a Whip in My Valise* and *White Thighs*, he also published a few serious writers, notably Beckett and Nabokov, who made Girodias a fortune in 1958 with *Lolita*.

Girodias couldn't see the point of *Naked Lunch*, but Ginsberg had meanwhile managed to get an extract into the spring 1958 issue of the student literary paper *The Chicago Review*, edited by Irving Rosenthal and published and subsidized by the University of Chicago. The ensuing outrage led to the paper's demise. Rosenthal resigned from the university in protest and started a new paper, *Big Table*. Issue one, in March 1959, included some more *Naked Lunch*; it was promptly impounded by the US Post Office, leading to a court case.

All this controversy made Girodias think that *Naked Lunch* might be an interesting property after all, and suddenly in July 1959 he sent round a young South African named Sinclair Beiles, who wrote counterfeit Chinese erotica under the name of Wu Wu Meng, to tell Burroughs that he had ten days to prepare *Naked Lunch* for publication. Beiles and Gysin helped to edit it, and at the end of July it appeared.

Burroughs had taken up painting, under the inspiration of Gysin, and he produced a calligraphic cover design with a number of Gysin-style lettristic swirls. He had already enclosed some of these in a letter to Ginsberg, telling him 'They are *alive*, these forms like living organisms.'[36]

Burroughs was instantly notorious, joining his already famous friends Kerouac and Ginsberg. He remembered a newspaper around 1959 – seemingly the British tabloid the *News of the World* – which ran a story about the three of them under the headline BLAME THESE MEN FOR THE BEATNIK HORROR. 'They had a picture of me in a suit, saying "he has the appearance of a Protestant minister or a banker, but actually he's very subversive, dedicated to subverting all decent values."'[37]

Burroughs wrote a further article about *Naked Lunch*, included in later editions, entitled 'Deposition Concerning A Sickness'.

The Paris edition of *Naked Lunch* (1959), with Burroughs's calligraphy: 'They are *alive*, these forms like living organisms'.

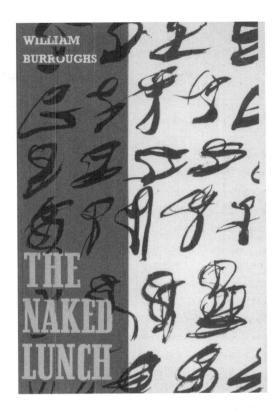

Somewhat moralistic, it dwelt on the horror of drug addiction and was intended to defend his position in case of further obscenity trouble. He said he had no precise memory of writing it, since it had come to him in a delirium of withdrawal, and discussed the drug problem, championing apomorphine and including an exposition of what he called *The Algebra of Need*, 'a basic formula of "evil" virus'. Since the book was about the hard drugs health problem it was 'necessarily brutal, obscene and disgusting'. Furthermore, he said, the apparently obscene hanging sequences in the book were in fact a tract against capital punishment, in the manner of Jonathan Swift.

Ginsberg was disappointed with Burroughs's 'Deposition', feeling it was unnecessarily cautious and moralistic and went against the real spirit of the book, but Burroughs was now caught up in both obscenity and drugs trouble and could hardly be blamed for wanting to cover himself. The aftermath of the 'camel saddles' business had reached Paris as a police drug raid on the Beat Hotel, targeting Burroughs. It was a particularly unpleasant ordeal since he spent the day at police headquarters going through withdrawal while they took statements and filled forms. It was probably the day he remembered ending at last with the word Pharmacie ('green neon letters in electric blue twilight'), washing down his pills with a café crème, and listening to an Edith Piaf number on the jukebox.[38]

Burroughs was addicted again. Ted Morgan has an evocative account of visiting Burroughs at this time from the American poet Harold Norse, who dropped in on him uninvited at the Beat Hotel after a stay in Italy. 'Don't . . . like . . . Italy', said Burroughs.

'Oh, I like the people, the sun.'
Silence.
'Hate . . . the . . . sun.'
'Uh, haha, well, *Paris* is great.'
Silence.
'Never . . . go . . . out,' said Burroughs.[39]

Dr Dent had sent Burroughs some apomorphine and he was determined to put himself through the cure again, in Paris; he had taken notes during treatment, and Dent's nurse, 'Smitty', had even given him a notebook with the necessary itinerary. All he needed was someone to be in attendance and help him. Being apprehensive of the psychic states that Burroughs might manifest during withdrawal, Brion Gysin didn't want to be involved.

Harold Norse recommended a nearby English-language book-shop as a good place to meet people. This was Le Mistral on rue

de la Bûcherie, at the far end of the rue de la Huchette, facing the
Seine and the cathedral of Notre Dame (since the early 1960s it
has been called Shakespeare and Co., taking its new name from
a famous Paris bookshop run by Sylvia Beach in James Joyce's day).
It was run by an American named George Whitman, who let young
travellers stay there in return for writing a journal and helping
around the shop.

One of the people staying there that summer of 1959 was a young
Englishman, Ian Sommerville. He was a tall, thin, intense young
man from the North, with a strong accent, studying mathematics
at Cambridge. He was up a ladder shelving books and he dropped
a book on Burroughs, leading to apologies and a conversation.
They soon became friends and before long Sommerville was at the
Beat Hotel nursing Burroughs through codeine withdrawal; sick,
ranting and all but delirious.

'Fuckin' unbelievable', Sommerville told Harold Norse when
he came to the door; 'I never want to go through this again, man.
Hallucinations, convulsions, freakouts, the edge of insanity.'[40] But
the weirdest thing, perhaps, was that despite their age difference –
25 years or so – Norse had initially mistaken Sommerville for
Burroughs. 'I'm a replica', said Sommerville.[41]

Burroughs and Sommerville began a romantic relationship that
would last into the 1970s, with Burroughs deferring to Sommerville's
expertise in mathematics, computing, electronics and gadgets
(notably tape recorders). He figures in Burroughs's books as
'the Subliminal Kid' and 'Technical Tilly'. He also managed to
get Burroughs's filing in order; when they first met, Sommerville
said later, 'he had twenty files, seventeen of which were labelled
Miscellaneous'.[42]

Gysin described Sommerville as being as sharp as a tack and –
in a characteristically mythomane detail – crackling with electricity,
giving off strong shocks of static with his handshake. Gysin had a
close female friend called Felicity Mason (despite his misogyny he

Ian Sommerville in the Beat Hotel; photo by Harold Chapman, *c.* 1960.

was a great charmer) and she couldn't actually imagine Burroughs in bed with anyone, so she asked Sommerville what it was like. 'Creepy kicks, man', he said (perhaps playing up to her question), 'creepy kicks . . .'. And then he laughed.[43]

Towards the end of *Junky*, Burroughs relates the new phenomenon of cool narcotic agents, men in deep cover who were in every respect hipsters except they were working for Uncle Sam. And now in the late autumn of 1959, in Paris, he encountered something similar when two men from *Life* magazine came to call on him, the double act of writer David Snell and photographer Loomis Dean. 'Have an Old Gold, Mr Burroughs' was Snell's opening line,

'Author William Burroughs, an ex dope addict, relaxes on a shabby bed in what is known as a [sic] Beat Hotel.' Photo for *Life* magazine by Loomis Dean, autumn 1959.

a reference to the Hauser and O'Brien sequence in *Naked Lunch* (doing the Nasty and Nice cop routine, Hauser would hit you and then O'Brien would offer you a cigarette; 'just like a cop to smoke Old Golds somehow', thinks Lee).

Burroughs had no liking for *Life* – the *Time-Life* magazine organization, considered as a control machine, later became a major *bête noire* – but he liked Snell and Dean. They were a couple of 'far out cats' with a real appreciation of his work, he told Ginsberg.[44]

Snell and Dean hung out with Burroughs for several days and Dean took some memorable photographs, including one of Burroughs studying a Gysin painting while wearing special glasses to see more detail. Burroughs exonerated them from the final piece, 'The Only Rebellion Around' in the 30 November 1959 issue, which was written by a staff writer and covered the so-called Beat phenomenon in general.

The article came to the attention of Burroughs's mother, who was appalled. Burroughs's father had recently had a heart attack, and she implied that his son's horrible life wasn't helping. Burroughs wrote back as reasonably as possible. He had read the article ('a bit silly perhaps . . . but it is a mass medium . . . [so] sensation factors must be played up'):

> In order to earn my reputation I may have to start drinking my tea from a skull since this is the only vice remaining to me . . . four pots a day and heavy sugar . . . did nurse make tea all the time? It's an English practice that seems to come natural to me . . . I hope I am not ludicrously miscast as the wickedest man alive, a title vacated by the late Aleister Crowley . . .

He reminded her that others who had held the title – Byron, Baudelaire – were highly respected now, closing 'Please keep me informed as to Dad's condition and give him my heart-felt wish for his recovery.'[45]

Just before Snell and Dean arrived, Burroughs had been in London for a further visit to Dr Dent. When the three of them came back in from their first lunch on 1 October 1959, Brion Gysin showed them what he had discovered in Burroughs's absence. He had been in his room making a picture mount with a Stanley knife, incidentally slicing through some newspaper underneath it, when the new juxtapositions of the cut-up newspaper suddenly struck him as interesting and funny. He had just invented the cut-up method, which would dominate Burroughs's work for the next decade.

It wasn't an entirely new procedure. It was related to surrealist language games, and Marcel Duchamp had already experimented with putting four texts into quarters of a square grid, as well as further games of chance composition variously involving musical notes or a dictionary. Tristan Tzara had famously advocated the composition of poetry by cutting newspaper with scissors and pulling the words out of a bag. Where the cut-ups differed from Tzara, however, was that they were not an aleatory means of generating texts from scratch, but rather a method of treating existing texts, which would bring out their latent and unsuspected qualities.

'Writing is fifty years behind painting', Gysin announced, by which he meant that it was time for writing to catch up with collage and montage (although abstract formalism with language had been tried, to some extent, by Gertrude Stein, and Burroughs saw Eliot's *The Waste Land* as a cut-up). Gysin's particular interest was less in cut-up than permutation, recombining phrases such as 'Can Mother Be Wrong?', 'Junk Is No Good Baby', 'No Poets Dont Own Words', 'I Don't Work You Dig', and 'I AM THAT I AM' (the latter taken through its 120 variations and broadcast by the BBC in 1959, to almost unprecedented listener dissatisfaction). Burroughs, on the other hand, could use cut-ups of his own work to produce an oddly wistful and often melancholy prose-poetry, finding new material such as

Sad movie drifting in islands of rubbish, black lagoons and fish
people waiting a place forgotten – Fossil honky tonk swept out
by a ceiling fan – Old photographer trick tuned them out.

'I am dying, Meester?'

Flashes in front of my eyes naked and sullen – Rotten dawn
wind in sleep – Death rot on Panama photo where
the awning flaps.[46]

The cut-up method soon produced two collaborative books, both
in 1960: *Minutes to Go*, with cut-ups by Burroughs, Gysin, Gregory
Corso and Sinclair Beiles, and *The Exterminator!* (not to be confused
with a later Burroughs book with a similar title) by Gysin and
Burroughs alone. The cover design of *Minutes to Go* resembled
a 'four quarter' cut-up, and some copies were issued with a wrap-
around band proclaiming, in aggressive Lettrist style, *'Un règlement*

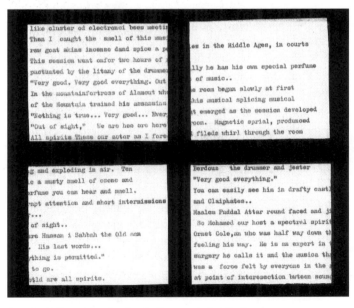

A cut-up by Burroughs, showing the 'four quarter' method.

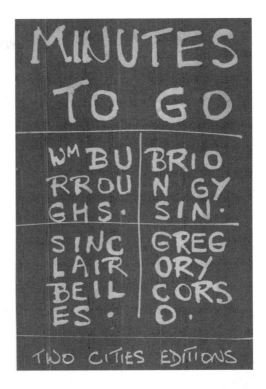

Wm BuBrio at work: the cover of 1960's *Minutes To Go*, like a 'four quarter' cut-up.

de comptes avec la littérature' (a settling of accounts – scores, even – with Literature). Gysin felt he was being under-recognized, and wrote to the publisher of *The Exterminator!* to complain he was insufficiently credited as the rightful inventor of the technique ('no literary bucking for place here', he added, 'Times are just hard enough as it is . . .').[47]

Instead it was largely associated with Burroughs. Girodias was now running a night club, La Grande Séverine, and he invited Burroughs to dinner where he met another Girodias author, Samuel Beckett. The two of them had a night of heavy drinking (Burroughs felt so ill afterwards that he became teetotal for a while) and difficult conversation. Leaning forward to make himself heard above the bossa nova band, Beckett asked Burroughs 'What can you tell me, Mr Burroughs, about this cut-up method of yours?' Burroughs explained it as best he could. 'That's not writing,' said Beckett indignantly: 'It's plumbing.'[48]

Burroughs was unable to remember much of the evening, but another man who was there, named Joseph Barry, reminded him Beckett had apparently said 'There are no answers. Our despair is total! Total! We can't even talk to each other. That's what I felt in *Naked Lunch* and why I liked it.' Burroughs had no recall of this, but he disagreed with Beckett that there were no answers. 'There are', he told Barry, in a defining disagreement between the great literary depressive and the great literary paranoid.[49]

In fact the cut-up method, in Burroughs's hands, was less like plumbing than sorcery, and this aspect would become more pronounced as time went on. It was easy enough to cut up a politician's speech, for example, and discover from unfortunate conjunctions what they were 'really' saying, but Burroughs discovered that cut-ups could also predict the future: you cut into

Burroughs lighting up in Paris, *c.* 1960.

the present, he found, and the future leaks out. He cut up some words and found, 'Come on Tom it's your turn now' for example, and the next thing he knew was looking at a headline that said 'Tom Creek overflows its banks.'[50]

Gysin was meanwhile taking a series of photographs of Burroughs around Paris, which was, he told Terry Wilson later, intended as a magical act to get Burroughs into the Académie Française. Burroughs also committed a magical act in Paris, somewhat under Gysin's influence, when he cursed an old woman who sold newspapers. He had a serious *Herald Tribune* habit, and every day he had to buy a copy from a surly old woman in a kiosk on the Place St Michel. He was always very sensitive to disrespectful service and implied slights (these would later infuriate him in London) and the old crone seemed to treat him with contempt, until eventually he told Gysin he was going to fix her. Things came to a head when a dog jumped up at his raincoat and he pushed it away, getting a snarling reproach from the woman. He felt a wave of hatred, and a few days later the old woman was filling a primus stove in her kiosk when it exploded and put her in hospital. A charred patch of ashes remained visible on the spot where the kiosk had been, and Burroughs and Gysin would sometimes sit outside a nearby cafe and overlook the site with satisfaction.

Dr Schlumberger could hardly keep up with this new dimension that Burroughs was slipping into, and the new psychic break-throughs coming from the cut-up method. Burroughs thought that 'raw peeled winds of hate and mischance blew the shot' referred to a shot of heroin, but Gysin later pointed out that it was about the shooting of Joan. Burroughs had started to refer to Gysin as his 'medium' ('talk to my medium') and his medium gave him a message that would change his life.

'Brion Gysin said to me in Paris: "For ugly spirit shot Joan because . . ." A bit of mediumistic message that was not completed

– or was it?' As they thought on it further, it seemed it was already complete enough. The Ugly Spirit had shot Joan *'to be cause'*, i.e. to cause something, to assert its controlling agency and 'maintain a hateful parasitic occupation'.[51]

This idea of the Ugly Spirit was Gysin's, but it increasingly haunted Burroughs over the years as he tried to make sense of his life. His full theories of words as viruses were still in the future, but you could hardly have a better instance of a word virus than the way this phrase – alive in one brain, communicated across the space between two people, then alive and controlling in another brain – took root in Burroughs's mind.

There is an old joke about a stammering sailor on board a ship, with something bothering him that he can't say. Sing it, he is told; if you can't say it, sing it. And suddenly he bursts out singing:

Should o-o-o-ld acquaintance be forgot,
And ne-e-e-ver brought to mind,
The fu-u-u-cking cook's gone overboard,
Left twenty miles behind!

It is oddly relevant to the business of psychoanalysis, sometimes said to be about getting things out and finding the 'the words to say it', and it was this joke that Burroughs remembered as an epitaph on what would be his last analysis. He told Ginsberg in an October 1959 letter that Dr Schlumberger had fallen overboard, like the cook, and been left several centuries behind.[52]

Several centuries is a long time. Along with cut-ups, Gysin had now introduced Burroughs to the futuristic, sci-fi style psycho-therapeutic movement known as Scientology. Scientological phrases and sentiments started to appear in Burroughs's letters to Ginsberg (along with a new coolness, now that Gysin was supplanting Ginsberg in Burroughs's affections). 'Hello – Yes – Hello' wrote Burroughs (a phrase from Scientology), telling Ginsberg he couldn't explain this new method to him until Ginsberg had the proper training. So, he advised Ginsberg to find a Scientology Auditor and have himself 'run', but at the same time, like a double-bind, not to pay any attention to this advice: 'I know you won't anyway, and it isn't written for "you" exactly.'[53]

Ginsberg wondered what was going on. He still hadn't met Gysin, and didn't until he returned to the Beat Hotel a year or so later, by which time Burroughs had gone. Gysin was very unwelcoming, giving an impression of great mysteries that Ginsberg would be unable to understand, and telling him Burroughs had left because he didn't want to see him.

In fact Burroughs had left because of those camel saddles. He had already admitted in a Paris court that autumn, truthfully, that the camel saddles business was a plan about cannabis, nothing more, and that even that had never been put into practice. His defence lawyer had said Burroughs was a man of letters (only in France, Burroughs thought, could that help; in America it would have made things worse) and that his anti-drug 'Deposition: Testimony Concerning a Sickness' addenda to *Naked Lunch* was about to appear in the highly prestigious *Nouvelle Revue Française*. Burroughs was let off with a fine and a suspended sentence.

Not long afterwards, however, Burroughs had a phone message from the US Embassy, calling him in for a talk. They reminded him that he'd been convicted of a drugs offence in France, and told him the French were planning to deport him. Meanwhile, they said, he should *keep his room clean*. Burroughs checked with his lawyer, and it seemed the French were not planning to deport him after all. But the more he thought about being told to keep his room clean, the more it sounded like another raid was in the offing, and the more he thought about that, the more he thought they might plant something.

In the spring of 1960 he left Paris for London.

8

Burroughs 1960–65:
Undesirable Alien

In April 1960 Burroughs moved to the Earl's Court district of west London, an equivocal, genteel-seedy zone (like those 'ambiguous, transitional' areas he identified in *Junky*), staying at the Empress Hotel, 25 Lillie Road. The Hotel is long gone, and the site is now dominated by the Empress State Building, a centre for MI6, GCHQ eavesdropping, and latterly the police. In what was establishing itself as a pattern with new locations, Burroughs initially liked London because he thought it was a place where people minded their own business. He was in touch with Sommerville but lived alone, and liked to relax by wandering in the highly atmospheric domain of Brompton Cemetery.

Burroughs had sent Gysin a New Year greeting card in 1960 saying 'Blitzkrieg the citadel of enlightenment'[1] and there was to be no turning back from the strange lessons of 1959. Now firmly under Gysin's influence, Burroughs plunged relentlessly onwards with his psychic voyaging and cut-ups, seen by some as a descent into madness and unreadability. Along cut-ups and drugs, another weapon for the citadel blitzkrieg appeared around this time with strobo-scopic flicker, in the form of Gysin's celebrated 'Dreammachine'.

Travelling down a French road by bus in 1958, Gysin suddenly experienced a near-mystical 'storm of colour' triggered by the inter-mittent, flashing shadows of the regularly planted trees that used to be a familiar feature of French roads (Cyril Connolly recalled 'the plane trees going sha-sha-sha through the open window . . .'[2]).

He told Burroughs about the experience and Burroughs later lent him a book that made sense of it, W. Gray Walter's classic *The Living Brain* (1957). Walter was a neurophysiologist who had been experimenting with stroboscopes since the 1940s, using them to interact with the intrinsic rhythms of the brain such as the alpha wave, at eight to thirteen cycles per second. Aldous Huxley also discusses flicker as 'an aid to visionary experience' in his 1956 book *Heaven and Hell*.[3]

'Flicker' or stroboscopic light proved to have a long and surprising history: Ptolemy noticed that spinning a spoked wheel between an observer and the sun could bring on visual patterns and euphoria, and Nostradamus is said to have waved his fingers across the closed eyelids of Catherine de Medici to give her visions. Gysin was able to talk the experience up, suggesting that St Paul's conversion on the road to Damascus – seeing the Biblical 'light from heaven' – may have been a flicker effect, perhaps giving him visions of crosses.

Along with patterns and crosses, flicker is prone to induce characteristically 'hypnagogic' imagery in susceptible subjects, comparable to the visions of overtiredness or the frontiers of sleep. One of Gray Walter's subjects saw 'a procession of little men with their hats pulled down over their eyes moving diagonally across the field', and Gysin reported 'science fiction dreams, I've imagined that I was swimming over what seemed to be an ocean bottom and that big molluscs at the bottom opened up and through them appeared swimmers in Leonardo da Vinci-type helmets, and a lot of dreams about fights between them.'[4]

With his flair for mathematics and gadgets, it was easy for Ian Sommerville to invent a low-tech strobe of the necessary frequency, and in February 1960 he wrote to Gysin that he had made a 'simple flicker machine' using a suspended lightbulb in a slotted cardboard cylinder that revolved on a 78 rpm record deck, from which he obtained beautiful kaleidoscopic effects through his closed eyes.

Gysin duly built such a machine, following Sommerville's instructions, and in July 1961 he patented it in his own name, receiving French patent no. 868281 for 'an apparatus for the production of artistic visual sensations'.[5]

Gysin had great hopes for the 'Dreammachine', not least financial. Among the rich women he cultivated he managed to get a machine displayed in Helena Rubinstein's shop window, and Peggy Guggenheim was enthusiastic until her artistic adviser Alfred Barr dissuaded her. The Philips electrical company were also interested, but the prospect of flicker machines in 1960s living rooms, like lava lamps, diminished when Philips discovered they could cause epilepsy. Even Paul Bowles's sardonic expectation of dream machines as 'a new kick for the juvenile delinquents'[6] came to nothing.

Burroughs was nevertheless impressed, and as John Geiger has noted in his superb short book on the subject, *Chapel of Extreme Experience*, flicker-induced imagery figures in his books of the early 1960s, notably *The Ticket that Exploded* and *Nova Express*. The Burrovian mindscapes of *Ticket* include the 'neighborhood of the flicker ghosts' and passages such as

> Pools and canals reflected grey suits carrying umbrellas – flickering over swimming boys as the magnetic silver light popped sound and image flakes – color writing a composite garden – layers peel off red yellow blue pools reflecting translucent beings with flower hula hoops naked in blue twilight . . . flicker cylinders spilled light and talk and music across the water.[7]

Timothy Leary was meanwhile exploring drugs at Harvard, after an experience with magic mushrooms in 1960, and had begun to evangelize for hallucinogens. Ginsberg was in touch with him, and Aldous Huxley – evidently responding to an inquiry made on Burroughs's behalf – wrote back to Ginsberg from Switzerland on 8 January 1961 to say 'I would think that Burroughs's best bet would be to write to the discoverer of psilocybin, Dr Albert Hoffman . . . asking if he can arrange for him, as an imaginative author, to test the drug experimentally.' He added that very useful work was being done with LSD, 'leading to deep self-discovery'.[8]

Ginsberg urged Leary to get Burroughs interested in psilocybin: 'He knows more about drugs than anyone alive.'[9] Leary wrote to Burroughs in January 1961, and Burroughs replied to say he would be interested in trying mushrooms and writing it up, as he had already with mescaline: 'I think the wider use of these drugs would lead to better conditions at all levels. Perhaps whole areas of neurosis could be mapped and eradicated . . .'.[10]

The states, places or mindscapes reached by certain drugs often have something quite consistent and recognizable about them. When British anthropologist Geoffrey Gorer took mescaline in the 1930s there was already something oddly Burrovian about it, with a

Cheap *exposition coloniale* effect, luminous fountains, etc. . . . Trams pass as red lightnings . . . Motor-bike revolving lighthouses . . . Cheap and ugly version of heaven . . . always luminous fun fair . . . Klee almost certainly uses or has used mescaline . . . As limited as if living in a colour film . . . Like the idea of heaven of a jazz-band leader – vague reminiscences of sugary jazz tunes – I am sorry for people who would like it . . . [11]

At the same time it is no less a truism about drugs, particularly psychedelics, to say that they vary with the setting and the individual, and here Burroughs's experiences were distinctive. He had a terrible time. He tried psilocybin in March 1961 and had unpleasant visions of green boys with purple fungoid gills. A month or so later he tried DMT, or dimethyltryptamine, which was even worse, with painful visions of white-hot ovens.[12]

In the late summer of 1961 Leary and several of the more-or-less Beat crowd were in Tangier, including Burroughs, Ginsberg and Corso, along with their friends Ansen and Sommerville. It was a would-be psychedelic summer, an insider's rehearsal for the events of a few years later. 'Leary arrived and laid us all low with mushrooms,' Sommerville reported, ' . . . and universal love reared its ugly head.'[13]

This wasn't what reared its head for Burroughs. As Leary remembered it, half memory and half parody, Burroughs reeled back, hand on his haggard sweating face, and said

> I would like to sound a word of warning. I'm not feeling too well. I was struck by juxtaposition of purple fire mushroomed from the pain banks. Urgent warning . . . I'm going to take some apomorphine. One of the nastiest cases ever processed by this department.
>
> You fellows go down to the fair and see film and brain waves tuning in on soulless insect people.[14]

Burroughs didn't like hallucinogens, and he wrote to Leary to tell him they were dangerous, DMT being particularly unpleasant. 'While I have described the experience in allegorical terms it was completely real and involved unendurable pain':

> . . . fire through the blood: photo falling – word falling – break-through in gray room – towers open fire – a blast of pain and hate shook the room as the shot of Dim.N hit and I was captured in enemy territory power of Sammy the Butcher
>
> The ovens closed round me glowing metal lattice in purple and blue and pink screening burning flash flesh under meat cleaver of Sammy the Butcher and pitiless insect eyes of white-hot crab creatures of the ovens.
>
> [. . .] white hot metal lattice in this soulless place of the insect people.[15]

Burroughs's bad drug trips with DMT and psilocybin fed into the landscapes of his work, particularly the land of Minraud in *Nova Express*, with its brass and copper streets, its insect and crustacean people, and its torturing ovens. Leary later gave a description of Burroughs's larger position in *The Psychedelic Review*:

> Burroughs was working at that time on a theory of neurological geography – certain cortical areas were heavenly, other areas were diabolical. Like explorers moving into a new continent, it was important to map out the friendly areas and the hostile. In Burroughs' pharmacological cartography, DMT propelled the voyager into strange and decidedly unfriendly territory.[16]

Despite his lack of sympathy with hallucinogenic drugs ('flung into science fiction paranoia', as Leary put it) Burroughs agreed to participate in Leary's Harvard programme to the extent of appearing in a September 1961 conference discussion at the Statler Hotel in New York, but he refused to take any more psilocybin, and in the course of staying around Leary's outfit for a couple of months he found they were incompatible. As Ted Morgan puts it, Burroughs hadn't come 'to listen to blatherings about love and cosmic unity. He wanted to talk about neurological implants and brain wave generators' (i.e. flicker machines). Moreover, 'He was not using heroin then . . . but he was using a lot of gin and tonic.'[17]

They were on a very different wavelength. Burroughs and Leary eventually resumed their friendship, but for now Burroughs wrote to Ginsberg 'I hope never to set eyes on that horse's ass again'; he'd had enough of 'Leary and his pestiferous project'.[18] The divergence between Burroughs and Leary would be an early 1960s watershed: Burroughs becomes a major counter-cultural figure, but he is not in tune with love and peace and he keeps his tie on.

Inevitably, Burroughs had urged apomorphine on Leary – who wasn't interested – and no less characteristically he had suggested the cut-up technique as a drugless high. In Leary's impression:

> . . . hallucinogen drug bottle and smoke pictures of strange places and states of being some familiar some alien as the separation word beautiful and ugly spirits blossom in the brain like Chinese flowers in some lethal blossoms bottle genie of appalling conditions hatch cosmographies and legends spill through mind screen movies . . .[19]

The day after his bad trip in Tangier, Burroughs started experimenting with collages; something which would eventually fill many scrapbooks. Like Joseph Cornell, the artist of surrealistic assemblages in boxes, Burroughs was an artist of associations and associative complexes, or as Cornell wrote of himself:

> Creative filing
> Creative arranging
> As poetics
> As technique
> As joyous creation[20]

Burroughs was very aware of the power in certain juxtapositions and given co-ordinates, like his train whistles and burning leaves, which he thought of in terms of Proustian effects and 'lines of association'.[21] In a particularly important 1965 *Paris Review* interview he talks of exploring 'how word and image get around on very, very complex association lines':

> I do a lot of exercises in what I call time travel, in taking co-ordinates, such as what I photographed on the train, what I was thinking about at the time, what I was reading and what I wrote;

all of this to see how completely I can project myself back to that one point in time.[22]

There is a related perception in Jean Cocteau – another man who liked to alter his mind at will, using opium – when he writes: '*Les Enfants Terribles* was written under the obsession of "Make Believe" from *Show Boat*: those who like this book should buy the record and read the book while playing it.'[23]

Along with the cut-up technique, Burroughs's collages were part of a larger assemblage aesthetic, sometimes seen as schizoid but also the dominant art form of the mid-twentieth century. Through the early 1960s there seemed to be almost nothing that Burroughs believed the cut-ups couldn't do. They could create a prose-poetry, but they could also be a kind of psychotherapy, capable not only of making new associations but breaking down old, bad, conditioned associations to wear them out and erase them, rubbing out the word to give a more silent and immediate perception. They could give insights into what a text or person was 'really' saying, and they could even give predictions of the future.

This random clairvoyance gave cut-ups an oracular quality, sometimes found in stray radio signals and the playing back of blank tapes. Burroughs had several radios tuned to static at the time Leary visited him in Tangier, and he later became interested in the 'electronic voice phenomena' of Konstantin Raudive and others, heard on blank tape. These voices, sometimes said to come from the dead, seem to come from a tendency to impose recognizable patterns on random sensory data. Burroughs wrote an essay on the subject, 'It Belongs to the Cucumbers' (the title is one of the utterances heard), relating it to cut-ups and tape recorder experiments made by Gysin and Sommerville; he also mentioned cutting up a text by John Paul Getty and finding 'It is a bad thing to sue your father' a while before Getty's son sued him.[24] 'You cut into the present,' Burroughs liked to say, 'and the future leaks out.'[25]

In August 1962 the British publisher John Calder organized an International Literary Conference at the Edinburgh Festival, attended by 70-odd writers. The Conference turned into a running dispute between conventional writers such as Rebecca West, Stephen Spender and Vita Sackville-West on the one hand, and more radical writers such as Alexander Trocchi and Burroughs on the other.

Burroughs outlined his programme as it then stood, explaining that he was 'acting as a mapmaker, an explorer of psychic areas'.[26] He outlined the 'new mythology . . . for the Space Age' that he was writing in *The Soft Machine* (the title refers to the human body) and *The Ticket That Exploded*, two books which would be completed by *Nova Express* to become the so-called 'Cut-Up' or 'Nova' Trilogy. Burroughs's mythology involves a new vision of heaven and hell: heaven is total freedom (from everything, including not only control and authority but all past conditioning, addictions and compulsive desires) and hell is being 'in enemy hands' or being controlled (again, by anything, but notably addictions and conditioning). The Nova Trilogy features the science-fiction style occupation of Earth by the Nova Mob, a gang of intergalactic criminals who promote and feed off mankind's addictions such as sex, language and power. The only hope of saving the planet lies with agent Burroughs, working as Inspector J. Lee of the Nova Police, combating the evil with cut-ups and apomorphine.

Burroughs also spoke against censorship at Edinburgh, pointed out the links between advertising and sexuality in consumer society, and outlined the cut-up method and its near-relative, the 'fold-in' method, insisting that there was nothing gratuitously arbitrary or Dadaist about them. Despite his rigorous and almost painfully sincere exposition of his work, some delegates believed the cut-up technique must be a hoax. Colin MacInnes, while sympathetic, raised the issue of Burroughs's mental health, and Stephen Spender suggested that, although Burroughs was making his method sound modern and even scientific, 'It sounds to me like a rather mediaeval form of magic.'[27]

Burroughs had stolen the conference, and indeed taken it 'into orbit' as *The Scotsman* newspaper put it,[28] but he remained intensely controversial. In November 1963 the *Times Literary Supplement* reviewed *Naked Lunch*, *The Soft Machine*, *The Ticket That Exploded* and *Dead Fingers Talk* together under the headline 'UGH . . .'. 'Glug glug. It tastes disgusting', said the anonymous reviewer, John Willets,[29] provoking the longest correspondence in the paper's history. After some initial pieties from John Calder around 35 letters followed, including a twittering attack by Edith Sitwell ('I can scarcely be accused of shirking reality, but I do not wish to spend the rest of my life with my nose nailed to other people's lavatories. I prefer Chanel No.5'). There were defences by Michael Moorcock and Anthony Burgess, and a response by Burroughs himself, insisting on the moral message of his work.

In America, meanwhile, *Naked Lunch* was running into problems. In October 1962 printer Russell Halliday told Grove Press 'We are in receipt of your print order for the Naked Lunch by Bunngus [sic]. This order I am returning as I will not allow my name to be associated with this type of literature'.[30] Another printer was found, but in January 1963 detectives arrested a Boston bookshop owner for selling the book, and an obscenity trial began in January the following year. The prosecutor wanted to know why the book had so many baboons; Norman Mailer praised its literary qualities; Allen Ginsberg said it was about addiction in all forms, including addiction to power; and Norman Holland testified that it was a religious novel about Original Sin, much as St Augustine might write (an observation which seemed to offend the Catholic judge). It was ruled obscene in March 1965. On appeal, the Massachusetts Supreme Court ruled in July 1966 that it was not obscene after all, virtually ending literary censorship in America.

Norman Holland's feeling that Burroughs was in some sense a religious writer is borne out by the oddly Gnostic aspects of his 'New Mythology' and subsequent thinking. The original Gnostics were early Christian heretics, in the time of the Roman Empire, who believed that the material world was evil. The world of matter was a thing of darkness and excrement, and the spirit – in the form of light – had to be freed from it (as in Samuel Beckett's Gnostically-themed play *Krapp's Last Tape*, with the Earth as 'this old muckball', and the separation of darkness and light). Burroughs and the original Gnostics go further, with a bad or bungling God – for Gnostics 'the Demiurge' – in charge of this world, assisted by the Archons, his bad angel henchmen. It is therefore imperative to escape from Earth – 'Time to look beyond this run-down radio-active, cop-rotten planet'[31] – whether this escape is seen in spiritual or science-fictional terms.

The sense of a botched world is caught in Burroughs's observation that if he could visit our planet on a starship, his first thought would be 'I want to see the manager! Who is responsible for this mess?'[32] Burroughs's bad god is the head of the Nova Mob, Mr Bradly Mr Martin (his doubled name deliberately suggesting the fallen world of duality[33]) and Burroughs compares him, perhaps surprisingly, to the Christian allegorist C. S. Lewis's concept of 'The Bent One . . . this evil spirit that he feels to be in control of the Earth.'[34]

The result is a centrally ascetic theme in Burroughs's work. 'WHAT SCARED YOU ALL INTO TIME? WHAT SCARED YOU ALL INTO YOUR BODIES? INTO SHIT FOREVER?' So Burroughs asks Ginsberg in *The Yage Letters*[35] repeating the questions in the early sections of *Nova Express*, 'Last Words' and 'Prisoners Come Out', the prisoners being prisoners of the Earth. Speaking as Hassan I Sabbah, Burroughs writes

'Don't listen to Hassan I Sabbah,' they will tell you. 'He wants to take your body and all the pleasures of the body away from you. Listen to us. We are serving The Garden of Delights Immortality Cosmic Consciousness The Best Ever In Drug Kicks. And *love love love* in slop buckets. How does that sound to you boys? Better than Hassan I Sabbah and his cold windy bodiless rock? Right?

Getting in a swipe at Leary's drug utopia on the way, Burroughs continues – here, and in the related 'Do You Love me?' section of *The Ticket That Exploded* – 'Listen: Their Garden Of Delights is a terminal sewer – I have been at some pains to map this area of terminal sewage in the so-called pornographic sections of Naked Lunch and Soft Machine [. . .] Stay out of their Garden of Delights – It is a man-eating trap that ends in green goo.'[36] Instead, Hassan I Sabbah offers only 'a programme of total austerity and total resistance', blaming 'the word', or verbal consciousness, and suggesting cut-ups, silence and apomorphine as remedies.

It is probably the Gnostic extremity of this position (along with a related omni-paranoid aspect; Burroughs describes *The Soft Machine* as 'the human body under constant siege from a vast hungry host of parasites'[37]) that led critic Tony Tanner to suggest Burroughs's most significant and valuable aspect was his original 'demonizing of reality'.[38] It is significant, but not entirely original. Several commentators have noted the Gnostic aspect, and in a 1984 interview, asked his 'religious persuasion', Burroughs replied 'Gnostic, or a Manichaean'.[39]

Still trapped in the material world, Burroughs and Sommerville went to Tangier in 1963, initially accompanied by Gysin and Mikey Portman; Portman was a young public schoolboy and persistent fan who had attached himself to Burroughs in London. They lived in cheap accommodation in the native quarter at 4 Calle Larache and were hated by the local Arabs, who particularly despised Sommerville for his promiscuous homosexuality. Insults were shouted in the street and mud was flung at their door.

Burroughs's son Billy Jr was growing up listless, troubled and unlucky; the previous year he had shot a friend in the neck with what he thought was an unloaded gun. In 1963 he went to live with his father and Sommerville in Tangier, but the visit was not a success. Billy disappointed his father by seeming to have no curiosity or excitement about Morocco, or anything else. Billy in turn was initially struck by the way Burroughs seemed to dress like a bank clerk. Burroughs had hoped they might rekindle their father-son relationship, but there was little rapport.

One night, listening to Billy occupying himself with his guitar alone in the next room, Burroughs suddenly felt like weeping. After six months Billy went home again, away from his father and his slightly sordid friends, gamely saying 'I'm sure this' – i.e. Tangier – 'is where I'll end up.'[40] It was typical of his inept, jinxed existence that he also managed to get into drugs trouble and further antagonized the Arab neighbours by going up on the rooftop, a taboo level traditionally reserved for women.

Burroughs and his books were still very controversial through this period. Keeping up the fine old tradition of protecting the public from itself, Her Majesty's Customs pounced on Barry Miles at Dover in 1965 and confiscated a dozen copies of *Ticket That Exploded* for destruction.[41] Burroughs himself had repeated customs and visa trouble entering America and Britain, where he was clearly regarded as an undesirable alien. 'Why have you come to England, Mr Burroughs?' he was asked on one occasion. 'For the food and the climate,' he said.[42]

Anthony Burgess's defence of Burroughs during the 'Ugh' controversy had referred to him as 'that courteous, hospitable, erudite, gifted and dedicated writer' and apologized for weighing in to the battle late, his only excuse being that he had been away in Tangier, in the company of 'the man himself'.[43] Burgess and his wife Lynne met Burroughs in 1963, and they got on well enough to keep in touch. In a London pub some years later, Burroughs asked

Burroughs in Paris, *c.* 1963.

Burgess if he saw any other writers in London socially. 'No,' said Burgess, 'they're all a bunch of swine.'[44]

Burgess wrote meeting Burroughs into the second of his Enderby novels, *Enderby Outside*, where Enderby meets 'a dangerous looking literary man' in a Tangier expat bar called The Fat White Doggy Wog. 'He looked like an undertaker, mortician rather; his suit was black and his spectacles had near-square black rims, like the frames of obituary notices in old volumes of *Punch*.' His voice was 'not unkind', but sounded 'tired and lacked nuances totally.' Fully in character, this fictionalized Burroughs is busy cutting up newspapers and juxtaposing the sections:

> Balance of slow masturbate payments enquiries in opal spunk shapes notice of that question green ass penetration phantoms adjourn.[45]

There is something about Burroughs's writing that invites parody. John Willets's inventory of Burroughs's world in the *TLS* was almost a parody in itself, 'a stereotyped debris':

> ectoplasm, jelly, errand boys, ferris wheels, used contraceptives, centipedes, old photographs, jockstraps, turnstiles, newts and pubic hairs

The Burroughs landscape is an unmistakable place, with its penny arcades and vacant lots, China blue skies, 1920 movies, a smell of woodsmoke and piano music down a city street, train whistles, frayed light from a distant star, rose wallpaper and brass bedsteads, ginger haired boys with red gums, deformed fish snapping lazily at jissom on the surface of a dark lagoon, and lesbian agents with penises grafted on to their faces, sitting outside a cafe in white trenchcoats, drinking spinal fluid from long alabaster cups.

Obscure obscenity is another Burroughs speciality, like A. J.'s cigarette holder in *Lunch* ('The holder is made of some obscenely flexible material. It swings and undulates as if endowed with loathsome reptilian life') or 'Mouldy objects, worn out in unknown service, littered the floor: a jockstrap designed to protect some delicate organ of flat, fan shape; multi-leveled trusses, supports and bandages; a large U-shaped yoke of porous pink stone; little lead tubes cut open at one end.'[46]

In the 1960s Burroughs's complex bibliography comes to seem less like the work of novelist than a prolific visual artist of some kind – full of sketches, variants, series, reworkings, experiments and treatises – much of it appearing in small magazines and obscure editions. In 1964 he wrote a manifesto in the *Times Literary Supplement*, 'The Literary Techniques of Lady Sutton-Smith'.[47] Lady Sutton-Smith is an English woman in Tangier, and as well as teaching a flower-arranging class at the local leper colony she likes to make her own fun with the cut-up technique

('I think of words as being alive like animals. They don't like to be kept in pages. Cut the pages and let the words out'). She gives an exposition of the classic four quarter cut-up technique ('cut along the lines and put block 1 with block 4 . . .'). There is no substitute for actually trying this; it can produce oddly apt and surreal results.

She further likes going for walks in her mind, and interests herself in modes of perception and attention, with intersection points, co-ordinates and columns of print. This was also manifest in Burroughs's collaboration with British avant-gardist Jeff Nuttall, who published a series of Burroughs pieces in his paper *My Own Mag*. The 1964 'Tangier Special Edition' featured Nuttall's drawing of Burroughs in a fez on the cover (trailing sinister cigarette smoke and looking like his 'International Sophistico-Criminal Mahatma' image[48]). Inside was a copy of Burroughs's own paper, 'The Moving Times', laid out in three columns: Burroughs was increasingly interested in reading across columns, cut-up style, and in the way the eye subliminally sees one column while reading another (the latter idea can also be related to his universal sense of impingement). *My Own Mag* also contained agony columns by Burroughs, 'Uncle William', 'Dear Auntie Homosap' and 'Bring Your Problems to Lady Sutton-Fix'.

Burroughs vividly remembered the day that the first copies of *My Own Mag* arrived at 4 Calle Larache, with its hostile neighbours and stones thudding on the door, because delivery coincided with a wooden object crashing through the skylight.[49] Burroughs was very short of money at this period, but finally royalties from the American edition of *Lunch* started to come in and he moved to a penthouse apartment, with porthole windows and leather furniture, on top of the national lottery building at 16 rue Delacroix.

It was a better area but Tangier seemed to be growing more and more hostile to outsiders, and Burroughs was ready to leave. Gysin was in New York, and in December 1964 Burroughs returned to America, where he had an assignment from *Playboy* to revisit St

'Tangier Special Edition' of Jeff Nuttall's *My Own Mag* (1964).

Louis. It is a nostalgic piece, as Burroughs searches for the pervasive yet elusive past of his childhood and takes black and white photographs: 'prowling about with my camera looking for 1920s scraps – bits of silver paper in the wind – sunlight on vacant lots'; 'I have returned to pick up a few pieces of sunlight and shadow – silver paper in the wind – frayed sounds of a distant city.'

> 'Ash pits – an alley – a rat in the sunlight – It's all here,' I tapped my camera, 'all the magic of past times just like the song says . . .'[50]

Rejected by *Playboy*, 'St Louis Return' was published by *The Paris Review*. Meanwhile in February 1965 Burroughs wrote a related piece, 'Last Awning Flaps on the Pier', an exquisitely melancholy fantasy of a swamp delta landscape where the houses are made from old photographs pressed into blocks, giving off a sepia haze in the rooms and streets, and where the inhabitants fish from fragile balloons flying a few feet above the water. They also sail the surface in light boats with sails again made from old photos, 'the pictures creating a low pressure area to draw the winds of past time'.[51]

Burroughs had read *An Experiment With Time* (1927) by the British aviator and parapsychologist J. W. Dunne. Dunne was particularly interested in precognitive dreams, and Burroughs found his ideas equally relevant to cut-ups. Time travel was an increasing interest, and gave rise to one of Burroughs's most idiosyncratic minor works a few years later, 'St Peter's Building (1888)'. He nominated a now demolished building in London's Soho – 24 Peter Street – as 'a doorway into the nineteenth century. Why this building more than any other building of the same period? Some doors open and some do not.'[52]

Burroughs stayed at New York's Chelsea Hotel before moving to a loft apartment at 210 Center Street, and 1965 was a productive year. In collaboration with Gysin, Burroughs assembled some of the scrapbook and other material published years later, after long delays, as *The Third Mind* (1978), with its close attention to cut-ups, coincidences and 'precise intersection points'.

Dr Dent had died in 1962 without apomorphine treatment becoming generally accepted, but Burroughs continued a one-man crusade, citing obscure studies to show that apomorphine benefited everything from anxiety to high cholesterol. It had become a panacea-like component in his mythology, with control, viruses, language and addiction on the one side and deconditioning, silence, cut-ups and apomorphine on the other. In 1965 Burroughs

Time travel: a building in London's Soho that Burroughs felt was 'a doorway into the nineteenth century'.

put together Number One (in fact there were no more) of his polemical and urgently titled *APO-33 Bulletin*.

Burroughs was suspicious of the *Time-Life* magazine organization as a giant control machine, like the Mayan calendar (a point made more casually by Allen Ginsberg in his poem 'America' – 'Are you going to let your emotional life be run by *Time* Magazine?') but he also had a particular grudge against *Time* because it had libelled him. A 1962 piece on the Beats and *Naked Lunch* had suggested he was a jailbird who had done time for murdering his wife; he sued and won, but received only negligible damages. In 1965 Burroughs took that 30 November 1962 copy and collaged it to make his own copy of *Time*.

This kind of creative defacement was very current due to the Situationists, for whom it was a major technique known as '*détournement*'. Burroughs's work has a number of intersections with the Situationists, notably in his sense that reality is constructed as a movie and we have to 'Storm the Reality Studio'; this compares

Dr Dent was dead, but the apomorphine mission went on: *APO-33* (1966).

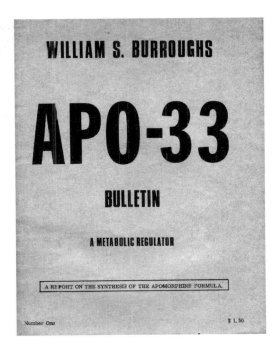

WILLIAM S. BURROUGHS

APO-33

BULLETIN

A METABOLIC REGULATOR

A REPORT ON THE SYNTHESIS OF THE APOMORPHINE FORMULA.

Number One $ 1.50

with Debord's ideas of the 'Society of the Spectacle' (which also led to Baudrillard's dictum that the Gulf War was really a movie). These ideas were 'in the air' at the time, and Burroughs pre-dates Debord in book form, but there are earlier links between Burroughs and the Situationists through Scots writer, junky and theorist of insurrection Alexander Trocchi, who knew both Burroughs and Debord, and the British Situationist Ralph Rumney, who knew Gysin. Gysin referred to his lost book *Memoirs of a Mythomaniac* as a 'detourned autobiography',[53] and Burroughs's *Time* can be seen as a detourned copy of *Time* magazine: similarly, the aggressive use of cut-ups is also a form of detournement, alongside their more surreally creative aspect.

Burroughs's feeling for surreal prose received a further stimulus in 1965 when a painter friend named David Budd gave him a copy of an illustrated history of the 1930s, *The Desperate Years*, which contained the final delirium of the dying mobster Arthur Flegenheimer, 'Dutch Schultz', taken down by a police stenographer after he was shot on 23 October 1935. 'Police mamma Helen mother please take me out,' he rambled, shot through the liver and running a temperature of 103. 'Come on open the soap duckets. The chimney sweeps. Take to the sword'; 'French Canadian bean soup.'

It was uncannily like cut-ups, and it had already been used in a book of parodies edited by *New Yorker* writer Dwight Macdonald, where he mischievously included it as a parody of Gertrude Stein. Burroughs was fascinated by Schultz's weirdly poetic stream-of-consciousness and he built a filmscript around it, published five years later as *The Last Words of Dutch Schultz*. At one point he wanted to change the title to *A Thousand Kim*, after what he considered to be Schultz's most enigmatic and haunting utterance, 'A boy has never wept nor dashed a thousand Kim.'[54]

There was a new departure for Burroughs in 1965 with the release of an LP record, *Call Me Burroughs*, issued by Gait Froge of the English Bookshop in Paris, which featured Burroughs drawling his way through pieces such as 'Bradley the Buyer', 'Uranian Willy', and 'Meeting of International Conference of Technical Psychiatry'. For the first time people could hear the stentorian harshness of Burroughs's extraordinary flat, rasping Midwestern voice, 'hard and black as smoked metal'[55] and oddly old-fashioned. In the words of the original sleeve notes by Emmett Williams, it was 'like a slow but faithful old Ford, with out-of-date St Louis plates . . . but hell-bent for interplanetary travel.'

It was also the first time most people had seen what Burroughs actually looked like. He stared emotionlessly out of the cover in those heavy black spectacles that had reminded Anthony Burgess of the frames around old obituaries. Starkly monochrome, with its sleeve notes half in French, *Call Me Burroughs* was a truly hip

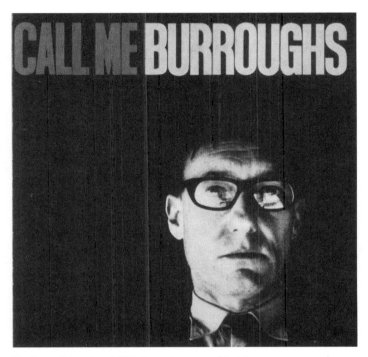

The face and the voice: *Call Me Burroughs*, LP record (1965).

artefact: the Beatles may have been the soundtrack for swinging London, 'but to the cognoscenti there was something even cooler to listen to'.[56]

In New York, too, Burroughs was suddenly a cool act. In April 1965 he gave a reading in the loft of an artist named Wyn Chamberlain, who lived in a former YMCA at 222 Bowery. The crowd included Frank O'Hara, Diane Arbus, Larry Rivers, Barnett Newman and Andy Warhol, among others; Burroughs was a star. This strange, sincere, conservatively dressed deviant had unmistakable presence, and he could hold readings and parties spellbound with his peculiar charisma. Panna O'Grady, a wealthy society hostess, dreamed of marrying him.

All this time Ian Sommerville had remained in London. Burroughs had asked him to New York, but he hadn't been keen. And now, in July 1965, despite his new success, Burroughs wrote to say 'I have missed you a great deal. Life in America is really a bore. Nothing here really, I just stay in my loft and work.'[57] In September he returned to London.

9

Swinging London, 1966–73

Burroughs returned to London in January 1966, staying at the Hotel Rushmore in Trebovir Road, Earl's Court. During his absence in America his relationship with Ian Sommerville had foundered, and Sommerville had taken up with another young man, Alan Watson. This grieved Burroughs, but he threw himself into his work, putting together scrapbooks of news stories and photographs with inter-secting associations and conjunctions.

Burroughs had a friend named Antony Balch, whom he had met through Gysin in Paris. Balch made a living distributing soft-core porn films from his office in Soho, but he had a serious interest in more avant-garde film and collaborated on several projects with Burroughs, notably *Towers Open Fire* (1963), *The Cut-Ups* (1967), *Bill and Tony and Others* (1972), and more minor pieces such as *William Buys A Parrot* (1963). Burroughs also did a memorable voice-over for Balch's version of the 1921 silent *Häxan: Witchcraft Through the Ages.*

Balch's more commercial films included *Secrets of Sex* and *Horror Hospital*, and he straddled the divide between the obscure and commercial (disastrously, as it turned out) with a short run of *The Cut-Ups* at the mainstream Cinephone cinema in Oxford Street. Audiences fled in droves, not just bored but seemingly repelled and disorientated, and the showings were remarkable for the quantity of possessions – coats, hats, bags, umbrellas – that were regularly left behind.

WILLIAM BURROUGHS narrates

BENJAMIN CHRISTENSEN'S

WITCHCRAFT
THROUGH THE AGES

X

AN ANTONY BALCH PRESENTATION

Promo booklet for Antony Balch's version of *Häxan*, or *Witchcraft Through the Ages* (1968).

Balch lived in St James's in an expensive block named Dalmeny Court at 8 Duke Street, sloping south from Jermyn Street towards Christie's auction house: rock star Eric Burdon also lived in the building. Burroughs moved there in July 1966, with Gysin following later, and settled uneasily into the area, shopping in Fortnum & Mason and eating in the evenings, often alone, at the Angus Steak House on Haymarket, a short walk across St James's Square. The British musician and counter-cultural figure Genesis P. Orridge went there with Burroughs and noticed how well the waiters knew him: 'All the waiters were foreigners and it was "good eeeeveneeng meeesteer William" and it was just like being with Mr Bradley Mr Martin.'[1]

Burroughs hadn't been in Dalmeny Court long when Sommerville, who had been working not very productively in a recording studio supplied by Paul McCartney, asked if he and Alan Watson could move in. Burroughs agreed, knowing it was a bad idea, and once again found himself the excluded member of a triangle.

Burroughs disliked Watson, who worked as a cook at nearby Scotland Yard, not least because he was very effeminate. Seeing builders playing football as he sashayed down the street, he would shout 'Score a goal for me, boys!'[2] and blow kisses; he would also dance on the tables in the Scotland Yard canteen. Back home, in Burroughs's suddenly cramped flat, he would annoy Burroughs by listening to screaming Maria Callas records. One day he was down at Hampton Court, catching the last of the autumn sun and listening to a cassette player, when he suddenly heard a horrible parody of his own voice on the tape, saying things he often said. It was Burroughs, mimicking him in order to control him, in what was intended as a taped curse to get him out of the flat.

This was hardly more than a rehearsal for the tape curses Burroughs would perform later, notably against the Moka coffee bar and the Scientology HQ. Burroughs was growing stranger and more

WILLIAM SEWARD BURROUGHS

8 Duke Street, St. James's,
London S.W.1.   Telephone: 01-839 5259

Burroughs's business card from the London years.

paranoid as the 1960s went on. He had already been disturbed by a cold sore on the lip of his young hanger-on, Mikey Portman, which he felt might be a point of entry for evil, possessing forces. On another occasion he saw a silvery light slide off Portman and hit him in the chest, after which he passed out: he felt this was a curse transmitted via Portman from Lady Pamela Frankau (a controversial, heroin-prescribing GP of the period who was opposed to apomorphine treatment).

He was also growing obsessed with coincidences around the number 23, which he explained to the writer Robert Anton Wilson around 1966: in the early 1960s, said Burroughs, he had known a certain Captain Clark who ran a ferry between Tangier and Spain, and one day Clark told him that he had been running the ferry 23 years without an accident. That day the ferry sank, killing Clark and everyone on board. Burroughs was thinking about this that evening when he turned on a radio, and the first news item was about a domestic aircrash in the States: it was a 'Flight 23' and the pilot was another Captain Clark (hence the phrase in Burroughs's writing, 'Captain Clark welcomes you aboard').

Burroughs started keeping note of coincidences, and found that the number 23 loomed up in many of them: Dutch Schultz, for example, was shot on 23 October. Schultz had earlier had a man named 'Mad Dog' Coll murdered, on 23rd Street at the age of 23. Schultz's own killer was paroled after serving 23 years. It all added up.[3]

Burroughs was growing more receptive to this kind of thinking as he cleaved closer to Gysin ('Talk to my medium'), while getting more distant and difficult with the warmer and saner Ginsberg. He had disturbed Ginsberg by asking him 'Who are you an agent for?'[4] The suggested, accusatory answer was Ginsberg's old professor, the staid liberal humanist Lionel Trilling, whose values Ginsberg was thought to have been imprinted with; Burroughs claimed he could even see Trilling in his face.

Burroughs also saw Ginsberg's father in his face, and his inherited Jewishness. 'Bill was thinking very much in terms of agents,' Ginsberg remembered, 'looking at me as if I was a robot sent to check him out . . . he assumed that everybody was an agent at that point. Not necessarily for the government at all; an agent for a giant trust of insects[5] from another galaxy actually. Women were suspect as being agents and Burroughs thought that maybe you had to exterminate all the women.' Barry Miles remembered 'When Bill was in London he was much more extreme. He might, for example, seriously argue that women had all come from out of space . . . it wasn't a metaphor.'[6]

The *folie à trois* that was Gysin, Burroughs and Balch embarked on another interplanetary adventure around 1968 when they encountered two people named Willy Deiches and Brenda Dunks, who claimed to be in touch with a computer on Venus named Control. This could be reached care of Deiches and Dunks at 282 Fulham Road, London sw10, in those days a rather seedy address, and would answer questions at twelve shillings a time. In this case Balch was the prime mover, or prime mark, and typical questions and answers included

Q. What is word?
A. Word is ETC
Q. What does ETC mean?
A. Electrical time control.
Q. What is virus?
A. Virus is B

Q. Is the opium poppy indigenous to this planet?
A. Yes.
Q. When did the Jews arrive on this planet?
A. Decades ago.

'Dianetics' first appears in *Astounding Science Fiction*.

Q. When you state that virus is B, are you referring to my virus?
To B-23?
A. Yes.[7]

Professional looking invoices were submitted, often adding
up to solid sums of fifteen pounds or so. 'Many of the answers
were oddly apt', was Gysin's comment some years later, 'quite
a lot of them were in fact . . . some of the answers were very
sharp indeed.'[8]

Around the same period Burroughs became immersed in
Scientology, which Gysin had introduced him to in Paris. The
brainchild of science fiction writer L. Ron Hubbard, Scientology

was a form of psychotherapy with the trappings and organization of a religious movement. Hubbard had launched it as 'Dianetics' in the May 1950 issue of *Astounding Science Fiction*, edited by John W. Campbell, Jr, whose editorial described it as 'a technique of mental therapy of such power that it will, I know, seem fantastic'.

Instead of the conscious and unconscious mind, Dianetics talked of the *analytic* and *reactive* mind. Instead of neuroses, the reactive mind stored crippling unhappy memories – many of them from previous incarnations – called *engrams*, and the central technique of Dianetics was 'auditing'. Instead of psychoanalytic free association, this simply involved a lie-detector-style electronic device called an E-Meter. The needle would jump when the person being audited was asked about anything that made them tense, but it was possible to work through these subjects until the needle gave a flat reading: when this was done sufficiently, the person was 'clear'.

Compared to the long process of psychoanalysis, the sheer crudity of auditing seemed to offer great things, and Burroughs felt it could do more in ten hours than psychoanalysis could in ten years.[9] When Burroughs talked about the murdered boy Kiki going away, he felt his hair rise with emotion, and then he passed out. As he came round, he heard the auditor say it had been a 'Rock C slam' – a very strong reaction – on the E-Meter.

Burroughs took the introductory course at 37 Fitzroy Street in 1967, then in early 1968 he took an intensive two-month course at Saint Hill Manor, the organization's castle-like headquarters at East Grinstead. He was fascinated by the process of auditing and put a notice up in Indica, the groovy bookshop run by Barry Miles, offering to give free audits. He worked diligently through books such as *Introducing the E-Meter* and *The Book of E-Meter Drills*; filling in a questionnaire in the latter, he answers 'What flowers would you like to grow?' with 'Venus fly trap'.[10]

At the same time he sensed there were things wrong with Scientology (the Scientological expression for non-members of the organization, for example, was 'wogs') and that in its pseudo-religious side it was 'just another one of those control-addict trips'. He had a particular problem with the figure of L. Ron Hubbard himself, and when he was asked the standard question 'Do you harbour any unkind thoughts about L. Ron Hubbard?', the E-Meter jumped. 'Yes,' said Burroughs, thinking fast, 'I can't help resenting his perfection.'[11]

Back home in Duke Street Burroughs had a Webley air pistol, and he used photos of Hubbard for target practice. The barrel was on top of the gun's main body and doubled as the lever to compress the spring. Burroughs pulled the barrel up on its hinge to cock the gun when something slipped and it snapped down, almost breaking his thumb: it was like a curse bouncing back.

Sommerville had no time for Scientology and he hated Burroughs looking at him with what he called Burroughs's 'Operating Thetan glare' (an Operating Thetan was a superior type of Scientological being, more perfect than the merely 'clear'). By the time Burroughs's course was over he was alone again in Duke Street, Somerville having left for a flat of his own, upstairs at 55 Red Lion Street, in Holborn.

Burroughs had a distraction from Scientology in August 1968 when *Esquire* magazine asked him to cover the Democratic convention in Chicago, together with Terry Southern and Jean Genet. The anti-Vietnam demonstration in Lincoln Park turned into a riot, and the ensuing police rampage fulfilled all Burroughs's worst preconceptions about the police. Ginsberg was there, chanting mantras for peace, and it really seemed as if America was on the verge of revolution.

There was also an extraordinary coincidence, or so Burroughs thought. Fleeing the teargas and batons, Jean Genet ran into an apartment building and knocked on a door at random, only to have it opened by a young man writing a thesis on his work (that was the story Burroughs had, anyway, perhaps from Genet; Genet's biography by Edmund White says it was a black woman).

By now, Burroughs's whole persona and project had ceased to be simply that of a 'novelist' or even writer. Instead he had become a revolutionary thinker, dreaming up left-field guerrilla tactics for the overthrow of society. Interviewed in 1968 for the underground paper *Rat* ('Subterranean News') he spoke of wanting 'action', and stirring up trouble 'for all the people in power'. Genet had told him writers must support the youth movement with more than words, and Burroughs said he agreed 'one hundred percent'; in fact he now wanted to eliminate 'the whole stupid middle-class' ('They are not alive. They're walking tape recorders').

The conversation took a characteristic turn when Burroughs said that all the important discoveries in electronics and psychology were being kept secret. He went on to discuss the power of infra-sound and vibrations at seven Hertz. Within a page or two he was expounding Wilhelm Reich, L. Ron Hubbard, and the possibility of the CIA pushing people under trucks with lasers.[12] Other inter-views mention killer whistles, camel endorphins as painkillers, and massive doses of vitamin A (usually held to be ineffective and toxic) as a suppressed therapy for the common cold.

Burroughs had various outlets for his thinking, including the men's magazine *Mayfair* and the underground paper *International Times*, where he published 'Electronic Revolution'. Other works of the period include 'Academy 23: A Deconditioning', 'Playback from Eden to Watergate', and the *Revised Boy Scout Manual*, issued only on tape cassettes in 1970 and dealing with subjects such as 'Assassination by list', 'Random assassination', 'Bombs and explosive devices', 'Chemical and biological weapons', 'Biological warfare proper', 'Infrasound' and 'Deadly Orgone Radiation'. The definitive package of Burroughs's ideas at this period is *The Job* (1970), a book of interviews with Daniel Odier recorded between 1968 and 1970.

Burroughs had long been associated with paranoia, but now reality was catching up with him. The 1960s were dissolving into

'The Age of Paranoia' (the title of a 1972 book from *Rolling Stone*, reprinting articles from 1968–70), and *International Times* offered a 'Paranoia' board game.[13] The watershed was often said to be the Manson murders, in which Burroughs took an interest, noticing that Manson had been involved with Scientology.[14]

Burroughs's embattled stance had its positive side in a guerrilla utopianism. Late in 1969 he developed his own dissident calendar, the 'Dream Calendar,' with months such as Terre Haute, Marie Celeste, Bellevue, Sweet Meadows, Harbor Beach ('the months have names like old Pullman cars'). It began on 23 December (or Terre Haute 23) and the months were 23 days long, after the Mayan calendar. Oddly beautiful but scarcely practical, Burroughs abandoned it after a year.

Burroughs was also committed to the idea of space exploration as the final frontier: along with a certain amount of crank theorizing and misogyny this was a dominant note in *The Job*. Space was part of the zeitgeist, but this wasn't the same space that NASA was exploring, with their earthbound 'aqualung' mentality: instead it was space as freedom from past conditioning, words, time and the body. The idea of out-of-body experience becomes increasingly important, and some of Burroughs's other pronouncements – that we need to leave the biological brain behind, for example – make no sense without it.

Smiling Bill: Burroughs photographed in Duke Street by Barry Miles, 1972.

Burroughs was increasingly thinking about revolutionary academies that would train young men in martial arts, guerrilla tactics and techniques of self-liberation, and this manifested itself in his fiction. He left the cut-up novels behind in favour of a return to narrative in *The Wild Boys* (described by Burroughs as a queer Peter Pan and published in 1971) and the related works *Port of Saints* (1973), *Exterminator!* (1973) and *Ah Pook is Here* (1979): the latter features the Mayan god of death and an evil American millionaire, Mr Hart, obsessed with the secret of immortality.

In *The Wild Boys* a tribal and homosexual youth movement takes on the world with revolutionary warfare, slaughtering American soldiers and lesbian commando units alike, settling Burroughs's scores with the straight world. Violent and sometimes sadistic, but intended as utopian, the book was of its time in its militant queerness (Burroughs finished it in 1969, shortly before the Stonewall riots) and in the very 1960s idea of the teenager and 'youth' as a new force. This new focus also allowed Burroughs to explore his own adolescence in the autobiographical figure of Audrey Carsons, a hybrid of Burroughs and Denton Welch.

Port of Saints put the Wild Boys back in time, setting them in the nineteenth-century West Indies where they acted as military advisors to anti-colonial black rebels. This kind of retro-futurism was a feature of Burroughs's later work, and in 'Academy 23' he had already placed the first Academy in 1899, with apomorphine treatment curing the world in the 1930s. Burroughs described these anachronistic manoeuvres as parachuting his characters behind enemy lines in time.[15] Seen by some critics as self-indulgent, *The Wild Boys* and some of the material that followed it was a frank attempt by Burroughs to explore, reify and publish his own fantasies, military as well as sexual.

Burroughs was consorting with the rent boys of Piccadilly Circus, the so-called 'Dilly Boys,' for sex and company at this period, and in 1972 one of them moved in with him. This was John Brady, a thickset and potentially violent Irishman who drank heavily. On one occasion he dropped ash on the floor, and Burroughs told him to clear it up: Brady went into the kitchen as if to get a brush, then smashed a meat cleaver into the desk where Burroughs was sitting: 'Light my cigarette', he said, looking crazed. In happier moments Brady told him stories of the 'little people' in Ireland, the leprechauns he had seen sunning themselves in hedges, and he had the gift – much prized by the master of the cut-up technique – of talking in his sleep. Burroughs noted down his Dutch Schultz-style utterances: 'Prince's gold is only old cock . . . load of monkeys.'[16]

Burroughs grew short of money in his London years. His books were not selling, a brief stint of teaching in Europe proved abortive, and around 1971 his hopes were briefly raised and dashed by a film proposal. A producer named Chuck Barris, 'King of the Game Shows', had made a fortune from a show called *The Dating Game* and thought he was interested in making a movie of *Naked Lunch*. Burroughs and Terry Southern were sent first class plane tickets to LA, where a chauffeured Daimler met them at the airport and took them to a hotel on Sunset Boulevard. Next day the car shrunk to a two-seater Toyota, and Burroughs sat on Southern's lap as they were driven to a dinner appointment where Barris stood them up; he had meanwhile looked at their film script.[17]

In January 1973 Burroughs was given an assignment by *Oui* magazine, to go to Morocco and cover the musicians of Joujouka at the feast of Bou Jeloud. Rolling Stone Brian Jones had already recorded the Joujouka musicians (*Brian Jones Presents the Pipes of Pan at Joujouka*) and the year Burroughs went he heard Ornette Coleman jamming alongside them. The music of Joujouka was a particular enthusiasm of Gysin's, who explained in a 1964 essay that the rites are really those of the god Pan, surviving into Islamic North Africa from the old Roman feast of Lupercalia.[18]

Burroughs went with John Brady as his 'spirit assistant' and *Oui* ran his piece in August 1973, heavily sub-edited. He had privately

experimented with cutting it up, and the result is instantly and
distinctively Burroughs: 'Then I caught the smell of this music
a musty smell of ozone and raw goat skins incense and space a
perfume you can hear and smell.'[19] As he said to Paul Bowles about
cut-ups, 'It works in the hands of a master.'[20]

Burroughs was still short of cash, and Gysin suggested they
could sell his archive; Gysin himself had been collecting Burroughs
material in a trunk for some years. Barry Miles from Indica bookshop, now a friend, catalogued it for them, and in August 1973 they
sold it to a financier in Liechtenstein, Roberto Altman. They took
it over in person and stayed the night – noticing the Rembrandts
on the walls and soaking up the mystique of discreet European
wealth – and they were paid cash, which Burroughs took away
in a briefcase before they split it.

Burroughs's years in London had been troubled. Several old
friends died, and he had family problems. His father had died in
1965, and his son and mother were both deteriorating in their
different ways: Billy was wretched, with a failed marriage and
drink and drug problems, and Mrs Burroughs was growing senile,
eventually strapped to a chair in a nursing home. Billy went to
visit her, found she barely knew who he was, and saw his chance
to have the contents of her purse. Suddenly overcome by the
bleakness of their situation, he began to cry, and she glimmered
into life: 'Billy,' she said, 'what's wrong, lamb?' In October 1970
a telegram arrived at Duke Street to tell Burroughs she was dead.
He had never visited in her later years, and he suddenly regretted
not having made more effort.

Kells Elvins was already dead, largely from drink, at the age of 47,
and in 1968 Neal Cassady died at 41, his health ruined by drinking
and amphetamines. Burroughs and Kerouac had drifted apart, with
Kerouac becoming a reactionary Catholic, and Burroughs last saw
him on his 1968 visit to Chicago. He later described Kerouac's life:
'First there was a young guy sitting in front of television in a tee

shirt drinking beer with his mother, then there was an older fatter person sitting in front of television in a tee shirt drinking beer with his mother.'[21] In October 1969 Kerouac was in front of the television watching Graham Kerr, the Galloping Gourmet, when he began vomiting large quantities of blood; he died in hospital a couple of hours later, in a textbook alcoholic death. The news hit Burroughs harder than he might have guessed, making him intensely sad and depressed.

London itself was getting him down, and had been for a long time. London was swinging, but not for him. The Beatles' *Sergeant Pepper* LP had come out in 1967, with its Peter Blake cover collage of People We Like, and among them, with figures such as Marilyn Monroe, Oscar Wilde and Stan Laurel, was Burroughs. There was a more esoteric tribute in 1971, in the Nicolas Roeg film *Performance*, when Pherber (Anita Pallenberg) is bathing the scarred back of the gangster Chas and says to Turner (Mick Jagger) 'Maybe we ought to call Dr Burroughs, give him a shot . . .'. But if Burroughs was admired by the hip and groovy world, he was hardly of it; he was still dressing austerely and squarely, occasionally giving up his tie for a polo neck (although Brion Gysin would insist on him getting into flares if they were meeting rock stars socially, and he also tried an unfortunate pair of platform shoes).

Burroughs hated the licensing laws and the British class system, and for him London was a grey city full of bad service, very different from the 'have a nice day' style prevalent in America. He took it personally, feeling endlessly disregarded and snubbed by shop assistants, like his autobiographical alter ego, Kim Carsons, in *The Place of Dead Roads*:

No the chemist didn't have a shaving *kit*, but he did grudgingly sell Kim a razor, shaving soap, toothbrush, and toothpaste.
'Will that be all, sir?'
(Gentlemen don't ask for shaving *kits*.)

For three months Kim held on at Earl's Court . . . three months of grinding, abrasive fear, defeats, and humiliations that burned like acid [. . .] Devoid of physical weapons, he turned to weapons of magic and here he scored some satisfying hits. He produced a blackout with a tape recorder that plunged the whole Earl's Court area into darkness . . . SPUT.
He conjured up a wind that tore the shutters off the market stalls along the World's End and went on to kill three hundred people in Bremen or someplace.[22]

As if revisiting a real event, he mentions the Earl's Court blackout again in *The Western Lands*:

Remember when I threw a blast of energy and all the light in the Earl's Court area went out, all the way down to North End Road? There in my five-quid-a-week room in the Empress Hotel, torn down long ago. And the wind I called up, like Conrad Veidt in one of those sword-and-sorcery movies, up on top of a tower raising his arms: 'Wind! Wind! Wind!' Ripped the shutters off the stalls along World's End and set up tidal waves killed several hundred people in Holland or Belgium or someplace.[23]

Embittered by unfriendly service, he fictionally adapts the Paris kiosk curse to London: 'The horrible old crone in the cigarette kiosk across from the [Empress] hotel who would shove his change back at him. . . . Several old biddies gathered in front of the blackened shattered kiosk . . . Gor blimey it's the Blitz again . . .'.

Having broken with Scientology, Burroughs carried out a sorcerous tape and photo attack on their headquarters at 37 Fitzroy Street in 1972, and felt he had succeeded when they closed down and moved (although only to a better site nearby on Tottenham Court Road, which they still occupy.) In 'Playback from Eden to Watergate' he documents another real-life attack on

Soho's once famous Moka coffee bar – opened in 1953 by Gina Lollobrigida, and the first in London to have the Gaggia espresso machine – where Burroughs felt he had been slighted.

> I have frequently observed that this simple operation – making recordings and taking pictures of some location you wish to discommode or destroy, then playing recordings back and taking more pictures – will result in accidents, fires, removals [. . .]
> Here is a sample operation carried out against the Moka Bar at 29 Frith Street, London W.1, beginning on August 3, 1972 [. . .] Reason for operation was outrageous and unprovoked discourtesy and poisonous cheesecake. Now to close in on the Moka Bar. Record. Take pictures.

Burroughs imagined himself standing around outside, and the Moka people coming out. If they did he would call a policeman; he had a right to take photos, and he could claim he was making a documentary about London's first espresso bar.

> They couldn't say what both of us knew without being ridiculous.
> 'He's not making any documentary. He's trying to blow up the coffee machine, start a fire in the kitchen, start fights in here, get us a citation from the Board of Health.'
> Yes I had them and they knew it . . .[24]

That October the Moka bar closed down. Burroughs knew it was his work, and felt the satisfaction of a job well done.

Allen Ginsberg visited London in 1973, and was shocked to see what a bad state Burroughs had reached, materially and psychologically. He approached New York City College and arranged some teaching for Burroughs, starting in February 1974. Burroughs left London around Christmas, not before time.

10

Holding the Bunker

New York was a welcome change after London. Other cities seemed to be getting worse but New York seemed to be getting better, and Burroughs found it 'one of the most polite cities I've ever lived in'.[1] Moving into a loft at 452 Broadway, Burroughs also found the fulfilment of a mysterious cut-up from 1964, 'And here is a horrid air conditioner'. The air conditioning didn't work and had to be replaced, after which he had three hundredweight of broken air conditioner lying on the floor; 'a horrid disposal problem, heavy and solid, emerged from a cut-up ten years ago.'[2]

Through Ginsberg he met a young man from Kansas named James Grauerholz; this was a turning point in Burroughs's life. They were briefly and awkwardly lovers, but it was soon over (Grauerholz found another partner, a triangle Burroughs was all too used to, repeating Ginsberg with Peter Orlovsky and Sommerville with Alan Watson). Instead Grauerholz became his friend, manager and all-round impresario, helping him with his writing and using his experience of organizing rock gigs to give Burroughs a financially viable career in live appearances.

Burroughs was 60 when he returned to America, and he was becoming revitalized by New York after London. The experience of giving well-appreciated readings gave him a new confidence and stature, although he still didn't enjoy teaching at City University. He prepared his course conscientiously, but he found some of the students wanted to see an outrageously evil figure while others barely knew who he was, or what they were doing in his class, and read comic books while he was talking; one or two became friends, but for the most part it felt like pearls before swine. He had a more fruitful experience of teaching on and off from 1975 at the Naropa Institute at Boulder, Colorado, a Buddhist foundation with which Ginsberg was involved.

Burroughs moved again, to 77 Franklin Street, and he was settled into a new life in New York when another blow fell, this time on his 62nd birthday. Ian Sommerville had moved to Bath, where he had a job as a computer programmer, but he had meanwhile fallen foul of a counter-cultural American in Holland named Bill Levy, editor of the underground sex paper *Suck*. Levy was nominally in favour of free love but Sommerville had angered him by making what seems to have been his heterosexual debut with Levy's own partner, Susan Janssen.

Levy guest-edited issue two of an underground paper called *The Fanatic*, and put together a feature on Sommerville entitled 'Electric Ian: Portrait of a Humanoid'. This included his love letters to Janssen, the information that he had a deformed penis ('Misshapen at birth', like 'a cubist painting') and a medley of quotations from friends and acquaintances accusing him of everything from being cavalier with money to having bad breath, featuring out-of-context quotes from essentially benign figures such as John Michell (author of *The View Over Atlantis*, with whom Sommerville had been lodging in Bath), Heathcote Williams and even Burroughs himself ('He wanted to be independent and now he is independent!')[3]

Brion Gysin brought this article to Sommerville's attention (back in Tangier, Jane Bowles had thought of Gysin as a sadistic alarmist who liked to pass on bad news[4]). Sommerville was distressed and distracted when he drove to send Burroughs a birthday telegram from Bath post office, and on the way back he crashed into another car. On Burroughs's 62nd birthday a telegram arrived from Ian

The fatal *Fanatic* (1977), the underground paper that Burroughs blamed for Ian Sommerville's death.

saying HAPPY BIRTHDAY. LOTS OF LOVE. LOTS OF PROMISE NO
REALIZATION. It was followed a few hours later by another from
Antony Balch, saying Ian had been killed.

Burroughs was distraught, and began to drink more heavily
from now on. Sommerville was an inexperienced driver and his
death was probably a coincidental accident, but Burroughs (and
Gysin) felt Levy's piece had killed him.[5] He later tried to make
contact with Ian by going to a seance, to no great effect, and
consulted Tibetan lama Dudjom Rinpoche (of the Nyingma-
pa, Red Hat or Unreformed school of Tibetan Buddhism, 'the
oldest of the Tibetan schools of Buddhism, but one of the lowest
in spiritual worth'[6]). Burroughs had an entree to the lama because
poet John Giorno, a former partner of Gysin, was now his secretary,
and he told Burroughs that Ian was in a bad way, unable to get
reborn again and stuck in the second level of hell.[7]

In June 1976 Burroughs moved to the celebrated 'Bunker',
formerly the locker room of the YMCA building at 222 Bowery.
It was an address with a history of artistic use: Rothko had had
a studio there. There was no natural light in the Bunker, which
was windowless, but Burroughs felt safe with walls three feet thick
and four locked doors between him and the street. 'It's pretty
impregnable', he told Victor Bockris, enjoying the fortress aspect:
'We must hold the Bunker at all costs.'[8]

Burroughs had an extensive personal armoury in later life,
including exotic and primitive weapons such as blowpipes. Taking
to the street in the Bunker period he would carry a cane, a tube of
teargas and a blackjack ('I don't feel dressed without them') and
he also had a steel 'Cobra', a whippy, weighted bludgeon that flicks
out and extends to full length. Burroughs said it would give him a
great feeling to pull a gun on a mugger, and despite his slight build
he reckoned to be pretty confident in confrontations: 'I don't like
ya and I don't know ya', he imagined himself saying, 'And now my
God I'm gonna show ya!' (from the 1920s poem The Wild Party).

There was a touch of the radical reactionary in Burroughs's idea of forming The Order of the Grey Gentlemen, a group of 'chaps' who would go out hunting muggers: 'Bill got worked up at this point. He was snarling and strangling his napkin, "So that if you see a mugger a second time, see, it's *onto the tracks* . . . And the Grey Gentlemen always leave their card."'[9]

There were film projects in the air around 1977, with interest in *The Last Words of Dutch Schultz* and *Junky*. The latter was the project of none other than Jacques Stern, Burroughs's erratic friend from the old Paris days. Stern wanted Dennis Hopper to star – or Jack Nicholson, or David Bowie – and Samuel Beckett to have a cameo role as Old Ike, the character based on Dave Tesorero (Burroughs had meanwhile had another meeting with Beckett in Germany the previous year, a rather frigid and decorous event with Allen Ginsberg and Susan Sontag). Now Jacques Stern was zooming back and forth in his wheelchair, like a man pacing up and down, with a syringe of cocaine still stuck in his arm, and he had Beckett on the phone. 'What do you mean, you don't want to?' he was saying, 'Well, fuck you, you old fraud!'[10]

Nothing came of the films, but something extraordinary was nevertheless happening to Burroughs. He was becoming one of the world's foremost celebrities, lionized by rock stars and hanging out with Andy Warhol. This involved him in numerous conversations with people who were punching under his own weight intellectually. Telling Warhol of a legend about Mohammed brought the reply 'Who's Mohammed?'[11]

December 1978 saw the New York 'Nova Convention', celebrating Burroughs in a four-day series of events. Organized by Grauerholz, John Giorno and philosophy professor Sylvere Lotringer, it featured figures such as Ginsberg, John Cage, Merce Cunningham, Laurie Anderson, Philip Glass, Frank Zappa, Patti Smith and Timothy Leary.

This period of Burroughs's life was recorded and to some extent organized by Victor Bockris, who put Burroughs into dinner situations for his book *With William Burroughs: A Report from the Bunker*. The result is Burroughs's table talk, with walk-on parts from the likes of Lou Reed, Joe Strummer and Mick Jagger. At times Burroughs can be seen playing up to his persona: talking of a possible acting career to Bockris and Warhol, he said 'I can play doctors, CIA men, and all kinds of things . . . A Nazi war criminal I could play very well.' Warhol instead suggested 'I think you should be a dress designer.'[12]

Burroughs is now more relaxed than he was when younger in addressing people as 'My dear', but the overwhelming impression is his earnestness, combined with flashes of black humour. As Bockris notes, Burroughs still has more than a touch of the 'insane German philologist in exile' that Kerouac saw in him years earlier,[13] and whether the subject is Iran or communism or cockroaches he is still grounding his conversation firmly in facts and pseudo-facts, still talking *about* things.

Back in London, Burroughs, Ginsberg and Sonia Orwell had been having a conversation in what Ginsberg remembered as 'that British manner, you know – light and polite' until Ginsberg said 'Let's *talk* about something!' Mrs Orwell thought this was very American, but Burroughs leaned forward and said 'Let's discuss something serious. Let's talk about *death*.'[14]

The longest single disquisition in Bockris's book comes when Burroughs treats him to around eight pages on incubi and succubi, sexual spirits that visit sleepers ('the demon lover, my dear!'). We can only speculate, says Burroughs, what further relations with these beings might lead to: 'You see, the bodies of incubi and succubi are much less dense than the human body, and this is greatly to their advantage in space travel . . . Now, we make the connections with incubi and succubi in some form of dream state. So I postulate that dreams may be a form of preparation, and in fact training, for travel in space.'[15]

Burroughs's discussion moves from dream spirits to out of body experience or astral projection, referencing a best-selling book by

Robert Monroe, *Journeys Out of the Body*: Burroughs seems to have attended a weekend course given by Monroe.[16] He had also been attentively reading some mainstream books on occultism, including Dion Fortune's *Psychic Self Defence*, from 1930, and David Conway's *Magic: An Occult Primer*, which he later included in a personal choice of Lesser Known Great Books.

Early in 1980 Burroughs went to Milan to address a conference on psychoanalysis.[17] Burroughs had been interested in Freud ('I have read practically everything that Freud ever wrote', he told Bockris) but now he felt he had gone beyond him, and he wanted to tell the analysts about Korzybski, Dunne's *Experiment With Time*, and Julian Jaynes's work on the bicameral mind. Jaynes stressed the importance

'No Metric': Burroughs in the Bunker, photographed by Victor Bockris in 1980.

of integrating the two spheres of the brain, notably the more creative but non-dominant right-hand side, and suggested that 'hearing voices' was hearing one's own other sphere, experienced by early and Homeric man as hearing 'gods'. In the event Burroughs found the conference disappointingly unserious; it put him in mind of an American conference of the Order of the Flying Morticians (a real organization; Burroughs had a friend whose father was a member).

Burroughs was in good shape physically, taking a vitamin B tablet every morning, going down and up four long flights of stairs to get the mail, and still doing his Hornibrook abdominal exercises, praising them to Warhol after Warhol said 'You're looking so good.'[18] He also had an orgone box. The main problem was drink; he avoided daytime drinking but was routinely drunk at dinner, and numerous photos of the period show him with his eyelids half down.

During the so-called 'punk phase' of his celebrity around 1978–80, surrounded by hangers-on and drug users, Burroughs also started using heroin again. A somewhat apocryphal story of the period has him going into the Magickal Childe occult book-store in New York, run by the late 'Horrible Herman' Slater, and appraising the newly faked *Necronomicon* (from the fictional book invented by H. P. Lovecraft, and in this version – the 'Simon Necronomicon' – including Assyrian gods such as Pazuzu, invoked in Burroughs's late novel *Cities of the Red Night*). 'After going through the pages and a few lines of powder, he offered the comment that it was "good shit." He might have meant the manuscript, too . . .'.[19]

Before long Burroughs was re-addicted, but at least it was better than the hell of drinking, as he wrote to Gysin late in 1980. Telling Gysin he was going to go on a private maintenance programme for his drug habit, he added, 'Whatever the cost it has been worth it to stop drinking. Drink has been for me a real curse and what a relief it is not to wake up not remembering how I got home or what I said last night.'[20] Burroughs found a maintenance programme with a Dr Karkus, which struck him as an inauspicious name for a doctor, and for the rest of his life he was supported on methadone. Ironically, this was the same substance that had held him in such thrall in Tangier as Eukodol: methadone is another name for dolophine.

Billy Jr was also having problems with drugs – he had written a book about his amphetamine use, *Speed*, generically in the shadow of his father's *Junky* – and more particularly drink. One of the benefits of teaching at Naropa, for Burroughs, was that it allowed him to be close to Billy in Colorado, but Billy was increasingly beyond help and felt further rejected by Burroughs's virtual adoption of Grauerholz. Now 33, Billy had a liver transplant and a colostomy, and in a suicidal act of self-neglect he stopped taking the steroids that kept his new liver functioning. He was found in a roadside ditch early one morning in March 1981, bleeding internally, and died soon afterwards.

A couple of years before he died he had written a letter to Burroughs but decided not to send it. He blamed his welfare existence on the fact that he'd spent his life 'doped up, beginning with an attempt to understand you . . . what in God's name are you anyway with your wretchedly evil entourage of bullet, gun, and mayhem *freaks* . . . did you answer a four-year old child whose mother you had just murdered when he asked, "Where are you going?" . . .' He signed off 'Your Cursed from Birth Offspring' and added a postscript to say that everything Burroughs had written since *Naked Lunch* had been 'tripe of the worst con-artist type'.[21] Burroughs found the letter when he had to go through Billy's belongings.

There is a vivid picture of Burroughs towards the end of his Bunker period by Edmund White, who interviewed him there in 1981. Burroughs was on form, demonstrating a blowpipe that he'd bought by mail order before tossing a cardboard packet into the air and slashing it in half with his Cobra. White found his manner somewhat formal and detached ('the Martian who's learned to be patient in his dealings with mere earthlings') and he was reminded of Susan Sontag saying that when you meet Burroughs, you think 'This is not a mammal'.[22]

Burroughs had completed *Cities of the Red Night* in the Bunker, the first book of his final trilogy. Featuring a virus plague, Virus B-23, it also includes an eighteenth-century libertarian-homosexual pirate community, based on the possibly historical reality of Captain Mission and his pirates; a missing-person private detective story with Clem Snide, Private Asshole; the CIA as part of an inter-galactic conspiracy; and speculative fiction on the prehistoric origins of the white, yellow and red races as aberrant mutations from the original black, caused by a meteor in a primordial 'red night' around 100,000 BC.

This sense of the white race as a freakish and evil mutation was a favourite theory of Gysin's, who disliked his own freckly, oatmealy skin as 'bad packaging'. The names of the six cities also came from Gysin, as magic words: Burroughs told Edmund White that Gysin had urged him 'to repeat their names before going to sleep if I want the answer to a question to come to me in my dreams. The odd thing is that Brion can't remember where he learned the names – Temaghis, B'dan, Yass-Waddah, Waghdas, Naufana and Ghadis.'[23]

James Grauerholz had been saddened by Burroughs's drinking and his renewed drug-taking, and left New York for Lawrence, Kansas, after which conditions in the Bunker grew worse, with more hangers-on, hard drugs and thieving. Burroughs visited him out in Lawrence, seemingly in the middle of Midwestern nowhere, and he could see the place had its attractions. It might be 'a nice spot for old age', he wrote to Gysin: 'feeding your goldfish in the evening in the garden pool, bats and fireflies.'[24]

In 1981 the rent went up at the Bunker, and Burroughs moved to Kansas.

11

Kansas 1981–97: Adiós Muchachos

Late in 1981 Burroughs moved to Lawrence, Kansas. He rented a limestone house south of the town before buying a single-storey, two-bedroom timber-framed cottage that had been built from a Sears Roebuck kit in the 1920s. It had an acre or so of garden at the back, and roses on the front porch. 'I know you think of Kansas as No-wheresville and think I am caught up in nostalgia', he wrote to Gysin; 'Really it is the other way around. The whole concept of place is dead and it's nostalgia to cling to it. Time was every creative person had to be in Paris, London, New York etc. That's all over and done with.'[1]

Freed from the handgun restrictions of New York, Burroughs was now able to indulge his old love of firearms, a passion supplemented by reading gun, knife and survivalist magazines. He owned a number of guns including shotguns, a Colt .45 and a .38 Special: 'Look at this,' he said to an interviewer; 'Beautiful, eh? My favourite, my Charter Arms 2" Barrel Undercover .38 Special.' Apropos of a Florida professor having been smothered to death with a pack of ice by three youths, he added 'I'd like to see some dumb fucker with a bag of ice get past that.'[2] Burroughs was able to share his enthusiasm with local friends like George Kaull, who had a pro-guns bumper sticker on his car, and Fred Aldrich; Burroughs spent many pleasant afternoons over at Aldrich's place blasting away at targets and refreshing himself with vodka and Coke.

Living in Lawrence, he developed a keen interest in William Quantrill, a Confederate guerrilla leader during the Civil War. Quantrill took no prisoners, and on the morning of 21 August 1863 he rode into Lawrence with his men and sacked the town. Anyone male who was reckoned old enough to carry a gun was summarily executed, with nearly 200 victims from fourteen to 90. It was still early when Quantrill's men rode out again, leaving the bank robbed and most of the town's buildings on fire. Quantrill himself was shot in an ambush a couple of years later, aged 27.

Burroughs's cottage was on Learnard Avenue, a name that struck him as 'Learn Hard',[3] and he continued to learn, evolve and mutate during his years there. In particular, an extraordinary new love of animals transformed his emotional life. When he moved to Lawrence he started to feed stray cats, notably a Russian Blue he named Ruski, and before long he had a whole family, with Ginger, Calico Jane, Wimpy, Mutie, Spooner, Senshu, Ed the albino and Fletch. It was Ruski, the first cat, to whom he attributed the saving revelation of love, which had come to him like grace.[4]

Burroughs's cats reminded him of people he had known; they were his past life 'in a cat charade'. He felt them as autonomous, struggling, mortal beings, and he found again the sense of essential *contact* that he had always sought in relationships ('you see the limitations, the pain and fear and the final death. That is what contact means. That is what I see when I touch a cat and find that tears are flowing down my face.')[5] Calico Jane was like Jane Bowles, Ginger could be Pantopon Rose, a madam from St Louis, and Ruski was Kiki.

People were sometimes taken aback to see how Burroughs talked to his cats, crooning over them. He could fear their moods: when Fletch was possessed by fury, Burroughs wrote 'I stand in deadly fear of his anger. Of any anger? The fear is in my chest, gray-black like underexposed film'.[6] One day he woke in tears after a nightmare of loss and regret; he had lost Ruski in a foul wasteland, amid sewage and burning plastic, with derelict roller coasters and Ferris wheels overgrown with weeds and vines. 'I shouldn't have brought him out here!'[7]

Burroughs's practical concern for the cats included a sticker on the front door to alert the emergency services that there were cats inside the building who must be saved. And when he thought about the nuclear holocaust, as he often did in the 1980s, he worried about the cats. When looters took to the streets, he said, 'I'll go heavily armed to the supermarket and shoot my way to the cat-food counter.'[8]

Writing himself into his last novel, *The Western Lands*, Burroughs depicts 'the old writer' fondling the *Audubon Society Encyclopaedia of Animal Life*: 'So many creatures, and he loves them all.' There was the flying fox, the fishing bat, the pallid bat, the Aye-aye, the ring-tailed lemur, the gliding lemur and the black lemur ('At the sight of the Black Lemur . . . the writer experiences a delight that is almost painful . . . the blazing innocence.') The old writer 'caresses the pictures as he turns the pages and pulls them toward him, as he's seen a mother cat reach out and pull her five kittens to her.'[9]

Lemurs came to occupy a particular place in Burroughs's emotional imagination, as a gentler and more feeling version of primate life; a kind of anti-baboon. Back in *Naked Lunch* there had been 'sad-eyed lemurs'[10] and now in old age he travelled to see the lemurs at the Duke University Primate Center, North Carolina, and sent cheques to support them: 'How I love them!'[11]

Lemur-loving pirate Captain Mission, from *Cities of the Red Night*, figured again in *Ghost of Chance* (1991), and the final words of the trade edition are an appeal for money on behalf of the Primate Center. Burroughs's later interviews feature a realistic and unsentimental concern with ecology and the terminal mess that *Homo sapiens* is making of the planet, particularly through overpopulation.

Ghost of Chance also included Burroughs's thoughts on Christ as a pernicious miracle-worker, and 'the Christ virus'. Burroughs's

Christ stands guilty of respecting neither quality nor animals, and instead serving the cause of the most worthless humans. *Ghost of Chance* was originally published in a luxury edition by the Whitney Museum of American Art, who asked Burroughs to tone these passages down or remove them, but he stuck to his guns.

He had already caused offence with *Red Night*: 'It's completely anti-Christian', as he said in an interview, promising the next book would be even more anti-Christian and particularly, in an American context, 'anti-Protestant'. So what was he to do, he said, go into hiding? – 'No, no, instead I go on a Red Night tour. As Napoleon said, "Dastardly and more dastardly and more dastardly is the sequence of success."'[12]

Burroughs's major achievement in the Kansas years was the completion of the late trilogy, the so-called Magical Universe trilogy, following *Red Night* with *The Place of Dead Roads* (1983) and *The Western Lands* (1987). *Dead Roads* traces the career of Kim Carsons, a queer teenage cowboy, and his outlaw gang The Wild Fruits. Kim is killed in a shootout back on 17 September 1899, but he is partly Burroughs himself, with passages of autobiography, and partly Denton Welch, whom Burroughs felt writing through him: 'It's table tapping, my dear. He's writing beyond the grave . . .'[13]

Dead Roads themselves are the places we will never visit again, except in dreams and memories. 'Remember [. . .] The road to 4 calle Larachi, Tangier, or 24 Arundle [*sic*] Terrace in London?' So many dead roads . . .'. It is likely that Burroughs isn't thinking of Arundel Terrace sw13 but Arundel Gardens w11, a terrace in Notting Hill where the disturbed poet Harry Fainlight lived at number 24 during 1968–9; he knew Burroughs and Ginsberg and had a brief liaison with Burroughs. His tragic death in 1982, while Burroughs was writing the book, was probably a stimulus to the memory of Arundel Gardens as a dead road.[14] Suddenly, in an impeccably Burrovian touch, a guide is showing a map of South America: 'Here, *señor* . . . is the Place of Dead Roads.'[15]

Dead Roads shows Burroughs imploding further into a personal world of fantasies, memories and obsessions: the Wild West, frontier outlaws, time travel, opiate drugs, occultism, handgun fetishism, revenge and science fiction, with an excursion to Venus. 'Johnsons' come to the fore in the final trilogy – the original working title of *Dead Roads* was *The Johnson Family* – and it consolidated Burroughs's long-held views on the essential wrongness of people who think they are right; people who are 'Shits'. Rightness itself was a kind of virus, and there was a Manichaean conflict between Johnsons, like the Wild Fruits, and Shits. The great moral value, if those words can be used about Burroughs – he was against doctrinal morality in principle, even celebrating the amorality of cats against the morality of dogs (the only animal apart from man, he thought, with a sense of right and wrong, and all the worse for it) – was non-judgementally minding 'My Own Business',[16] another long-held view.

Recommending a realistically libertarian history of drug use, for example, Burroughs could simply say 'This book should be on the shelf of every Johnson in America.'[17] The newer emphasis in the final trilogy was to give this a theological twist. Burroughs restated his Gnostic position ('To put it country simple: the Christian God exists. He *is not the Creator*. He stole someone else's work . . . The Christian God, and that goes for Allah, is a self-seeking asshole planning to cross us all up.'[18]) and he now contrasted the One God Universe or OGU with the Magical Universe or MU, 'a universe of many gods'. They were the Shit and Johnson universes, respectively.

Writing in the 1980s, this was strikingly in tune with Jean-François Lyotard's idea of postmodernism as a new paganism. Burroughs was particularly down on religious fundamentalists, from the kitsch idiocy of American evangelism (and what he called the American 'moron majority', aka the Moral Majority) to the rise of Ayatollah Khomeini in Iran. Well before the Rushdie affair, Burroughs saw that fundamentalism was at odds with any serious or worthwhile writers: the Ayatollah's script was 'nasty writing, Allah, and speaking for the Shakespeare Squadron, we don't like it'.[19]

The Western Lands again featured Kim Carsons, along with the old writer in Kansas, 'with my cats, like the honorary agent for a planet that went out light-years ago'.[20] The central concern was literal immortality, the 'Western Lands' being the ancient Egyptian Land of the Dead. Survival is seen as a difficult job, a task where only the few will succeed. This was another longstanding concern: Burroughs had already written that a hard-won 'immortality in Space' was the only goal worth striving for, part of a larger transition out of Time and into Space.[21]

This was more real to Burroughs than any questions of posterity, although in 1983, after much lobbying by Ginsberg, he was glad to be inducted into the American Academy and Institute of Arts and Letters. The applause, as Ted Morgan notes, was 'scattered',[22] even though by now Burroughs, with Beckett, was one of the two really towering figures in postwar writing. More than that, his work stands almost as a *reductio ad absurdum* of many of the concerns central to the American canon, including final frontiers, escape from matriarchy, male bonding, personal autonomy and freedom from control.

Burroughs also became a Commandeur de l'Ordre des Arts et des Lettres. Gysin, after considerable manouevring – Morgan depicts him kissing the hand of the French Minister of Culture's wife – was made a Chevalier of the same Order, which considerably gratified him. Gysin suffered badly in his later years with emphysema and cancer of the colon and later lung, but a friend, Rosine Buhler, remembered him at lunch in his final days, asking to have the Chevalier medallion brought to him and wearing it very elegantly.[23]

Burroughs saw Gysin for what he knew would the last time during a European tour in the spring of 1986, and Gysin's death in July of that year distressed him, delaying work on *The Western Lands* and taking away much of the pleasure he might have had

from the publication of their collaboration, *The Cat Inside* –
with calligraphic illustrations by Gysin – a couple of months later.
Burroughs wrote that Gysin was 'the only man I have ever respected
... His presence was regal without a trace of pretension ...'

> The only authentic heir to Hassan-I-Sabbah ... Through
> his painting I caught glimpses of the garden that the Old
> Man showed to his Assassins. The Garden cannot be faked.
> And Brion was incapable of fakery. He was Master of the
> Djoun forces, the Little People, who will never serve a faker
> or a coward.[24]

By the autumn Burroughs was working on *The Western Lands*
again, but there was a more unexpected development almost immediately after Gysin's death when Burroughs took up painting:
he had done some Gysin-style calligraphy in the Beat Hotel days, but
gave it up for fear of seeming to compete. Now Gysin was beyond
jealousy, and Burroughs further felt his art as a way of keeping
Gysin's presence in his life. He had experimented with shotgun
blasts on plywood since 1982, but after Gysin died he took up art
in earnest, and during a visit from the painter Philip Taafe in 1987
he discovered the pleasure of blasting spray-paint cans with a gun.

In 1987 he had his inaugural show at the New York gallery of
Tony Shafrazi, a dealer remembered for defacing Picasso's *Guernica*
with red paint. Burroughs found painting was 'a hell of a lot easier
than writing'[25] and that in a celebrity culture he could make real
money from it, but he applied himself with his usual sincerity. He
gave his television set away because he preferred to look into his
paintings, and his particular fascination with using a shotgun on
plywood was magical, believing the blast released 'little spirits
compacted with the wood'.[26]

There were new pleasures but there were old sadnesses, and
there was a strong undercurrent of melancholy in the Kansas years.

Burroughs had been feeling more tenderly towards his parents since his mother's death in 1970, and in 1976 he had published *Cobble Stone Gardens*, taking its title from his parents' gift shop and dedicated to their memories, with an epigraph from Edward Arlington Robinson ('We never know how much we learn / From those who never will return'). For some years he had wanted a copy of his mother's flower-arranging book, and he was pleased when a friend found one for him.

Burroughs remembered his difficult relationship with his father. One night in his twenties, under-employed after Harvard and helping out with the family business, he had gone down to raid the icebox and found his father there already, eating. 'Hello, Bill' he said, in what Burroughs thought five decades later was 'a little-boy voice pleading for love, and I looked at him with cold hate. I could see him wither under my eyes as I muttered, "Hello"'. And now, too late, 'I feel an ache in the chest . . . I reach out to him: *Dad! Dad! Dad!*'[27]

Burroughs began to look back over his life as a whole in Kansas, and it brought on frequent fits of weeping. In an otherwise fairly dismissive review by John Updike of Burroughs's book *Port of Saints* ('murderous claptrap'), Updike suddenly shifted gear to remark on Burroughs's wit, integrity and 'genuine personal melancholy. The net effect Burroughs achieves is to convince us that he has seen and done things sad beyond description.'[28] Talking to the British poet Michael Horovitz on the telephone from Kansas in 1992, Burroughs's 'sprightly' inflections suddenly became 'more wistful' and he went on to quote Edward Arlington Robinson's lines about 'mistakes too monstrous for remorse'.[29] Looking back, Burroughs was more and more haunted by a resonant line from Verlaine: 'My past was an evil river.'[30]

The really monstrous mistake – which he broached with Horovitz immediately after the line from Robinson – was the shooting of Joan; the day the Ugly Spirit showed its hand.

Burroughs had a fractured sense of self, and he felt something alien inside him: 'When I go into my psyche, at a certain point I meet a very hostile, very strong force. It's as definite as somebody attacking me in a bar. We usually come to a standoff . . .'[31]

This went with a heightened awareness of possession, and Burroughs was intensely ambivalent to it, like passivity: on the one hand possession was the worst thing, 'the basic evil', but on the other 'People don't have genius, they are possessed by genius . . . You are possessed by it. All you can do is make yourself open. Lay yourself open to whatever it is.' Warming to the same theme on another occasion, he said 'I remember what Norman Mailer said of me [. . .] the only American writer conceivably possessed by genius. He didn't say I was a genius. He said I was possessed *by* it, baby, like it was a demon.'[32]

By 1992 it was time for something more than a standoff with the Ugly Spirit; this time it was a showdown, with a Native American sweat lodge exorcism. Having originally been revealed by Gysin in 1959 'on a piece of paper in a sort of trance state', the Spirit had meanwhile come to stand in Burroughs's mind for America, and 'the Ugly American at his ugly worst'. It was 'very much related to the American Tycoon', to Vanderbilt, Rockefeller, and 'particularly [Randolph] Hearst', the newspaper owner and manipulator of word and image. Reprising what Burroughs had said, Ginsberg understood it as 'the whole of American capitalism, Rockefeller, the CIA'.[33]

The sweat lodge ceremony was conducted by Navajo shaman Melvin Betsellie, with half a dozen or so people present in a small space choked with smoke and steam. Ginsberg was there, naked, and Burroughs in a pair of shorts. It was a ceremony remarkable for its benevolence, unlike some Christian exorcisms, and the shaman repeatedly thanked the spirits and the participants for coming, before taking Burroughs's suffering into himself and battling with the Ugly Spirit. There were alarming moments when he appeared to put hot coals into his mouth, lighting it up in the darkness.

Betsellie said the spirit was stronger and more evil than he had expected. When he described it later, Burroughs said he had seen it in some of his paintings. The long ceremony left Burroughs exhausted and almost suffocated, but intensely moved: 'I feel it very deeply', he said afterwards, 'I like the shaman very much, the way he was crying. Deeply sad, deeply . . .'. Burroughs had earlier found 'various levels of persona' in himself – the phrase is Ginsberg's – with Dr Wolberg, but despite his liking for Wolberg he was sure this was something he 'couldn't have handled'. Altogether, he said, the sweat lodge exorcism was 'much better than anything psycho-analysts have come up with.'[34]

In his late years Burroughs drafted a fan letter ('I have never written a fan letter before . . .'[35]) to M. Scott Peck, whose book *Denial of the Soul* argues for the psychiatric reality of demonic possession. He also met spirits in dreams, some of them mem-orable: 'I once questioned in a dream an evil Italian mountebank spirit: "Like, who are you?" And he laughed and laughed – and went on laughing, in a marble dark lagoon, chintzy Italian decor – and he was deliciously evil.'[36]

After Burroughs's long disquisition to Victor Bockris on incubi and succubi, it is no surprise Morgan has him saying 'The best sex I ever had was with my phantoms'. ('People don't like to talk about it, but I've done a lot of research. There's one woman who had visits from her husband after his death, and he fucked her better than he'd ever fucked her when he was alive. He also gave her some tips on the market, how about that?'[37]) An increasingly manifest sense of space travel as occult-style 'astral' travel reached a logical outcome in Burroughs's Gnostically-inflected writing about 'Bodies of Light'. The human body, an obsolete artefact, was 'too dense' for space: 'However, we have a model to hand that is much less dense in fact almost weightless: the astral or dream body. This lighter body, a "body of light," as Crowley called it, is much more suited to space conditions.'[38]

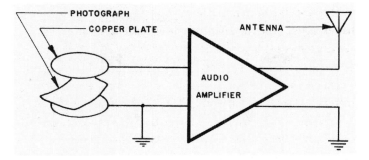

Circuit of desire: a wishing machine, as in Burroughs's 1986 lecture on 'The Technology and Ethics of Wishing'.

Aleister Crowley discusses the formation of the 'Magical Being or Body of Light' as the 'essential magical work, apart from any particular operation' in his 1929 book *Magick in Theory and Practice*, ranging swiftly over '*congressus subtilis*', 'the body of desire', succubi and the Egyptian Book of the Dead.[39] On a lower magical level, Burroughs had a particular *bête noire* in a reviewer named Anatole Broyard, so he put a curse on him. It seemed to work, and Burroughs decided to extend the practice to people who sent him unpleasant letters.

Burroughs became particularly fascinated with a magical device in a more modern guise, the so-called 'Wishing Machine'. He was introduced to this by a Lawrence acquaintance named Len McGruder, who lent him a book by G. Harry Stine called *On The Frontiers of Science*, with the irresistible subtitle 'Strange Machines You Can Build'. The wishing machine was a development of the Hieronymous Machine, patented in 1949 by a Thomas Galen Hieronymous, and it became more widely known when it was taken up by John W. Campbell Jr in *Astounding Science Fiction*; this was the same editor and publication that originally introduced the world to Scientology.

By the time the Machine came down to Burroughs it had simplified into two plates of copper attached to a small amplifier. Between the plates, the operator puts a photograph of a person they wish to heal, or some hair or nail clippings. One of the machine's pioneers had remarkable results curing his daughter's acne, and Burroughs spent hours with the machine trying to help Gysin's emphysema, to no avail, but seemed to cure a growth on his cat Ginger.

Burroughs used the machine for over a decade, and wrote it into *The Western Lands*. He also gave a lecture on it at Naropa University, 'The Technology and Ethics of Wishing', where members of the audience laughed – more at him than with him, although perhaps a little nervously in some cases – as Burroughs's hard, pragmatic drawl championed the device as not only a healing tool but potentially a killing machine, detailing the percentage kill rates achieved by working on photographs of weevils.

When it came to magical wishing, Burroughs quoted the nineteenth-century French occultist Eliphas Levi; the knack was to achieve a certain disengagement, as he quoted again to a friend ten years later: '*Souhaiter sans desire* . . . To wish without desiring'.[40] As for the wishing machine, the most telling point about it (as revealed by John W. Campbell and G. Harry Stine in their respective discussions of the 'Symbolic Hieronymous Machine') is that *a diagram of the machine works as well as the machine itself.*[41]

It is a striking instance of Edmund White's characterization of Burroughs's sources as tending towards the 'cruddy or recherché'.[42] Alongside Mayan archaeology, and popular genres such as Westerns and sci-fi, Burroughs was excited by Wilhelm Reich, Scientology, killer sound weapons, and the *National Enquirer*. Faced with the richness and essential reasonableness of Buddhism, he found more stimulation – as he says in *The Retreat Diaries*, written on a Buddhist retreat – in the New Age pseudo-wisdom of Carlos Castaneda, the best-selling ethnographic fraud. Late in life, having earlier been sceptical about UFOs, he became excited by Whitley Streiber's account of his personal abduction by extraterrestrials, and in 1990 he went to stay with Streiber and his wife in the hope of an alien encounter.

There is a well-known belief among 'primitive' people that nothing happens innocently or by chance; all deaths are murder, and the witch doctor can uncover the culprit. Burroughs joked about this in *Naked Lunch*, where the Amazonian Indian ('Primitive Man') regards no death as accidental, and the medicine man predictably blames a neighbouring tribe ('Take it from an old brujo, dearie, they don't like surprises').[43] But by now, and for some years previously, Burroughs believed something like this himself with his Magical Universe: 'The belief that nothing happens until somebody wills it to happen. There are no accidents.'[44] Consolidating a life-long belief in the irrational, Burroughs's later life ran almost entirely on pre-Enlightenment lines, communing with the dead, meeting spirits in dreams, sending curses, and being obsessed with weapons, including knives and even blowpipes; Harvard-educated, he had regressed himself into a postmodern primitivism.

Many of Burroughs's beliefs are easily paraphrased in psychiatric terms, but this doesn't explain their cultural significance, or why varieties of paranoia were central to the work of several American writers in the same era, including Hunter S. Thompson, Thomas Pynchon and Philip K. Dick. By the end of his life Burroughs was famous for the crankiness of his thinking, but his ideas on viruses and parasites, for example, make a certain sense. To some people they were a visionary anticipation of AIDS, and from another perspective they are part of his endless concern with encroachment, impingement and control, but they are also about the penetrating, colonizing possibilities of language, and what we would now call memes.

'Clear demonstration that we do not control language', Burroughs had jotted down on his Buddhist retreat in 1975: 'sub-vocal songs'. As he shaved that morning, 'Just My Bill' from *Showboat* popped up in his mind of its own accord, like the little obsessions and thoughts with a life of their own that were known in eighteenth-century Britain as 'maggots'.[45] Or from a twentieth-century authority:

memes should be regarded as living structures, not just metaphorically but technically. When you plant a fertile meme in my mind you literally parasitize my brain, turning it into a vehicle for the meme's propagation in just the way that a virus may parasitize the genetic mechanism of a host cell . . . the meme for, say, 'belief in life after death' is actually realized physically, millions of times over, as a structure in the nervous systems of individual men the world over.[46]

Late in 1994 Burroughs finished a dream diary-cum-journal-cum-memoir, *My Education: A Book of Dreams*. The years flashed by ('Morphine and Dilaudid scripts . . . Pantopon Rose . . . Old time junkies at 103rd and Broadway') and his dreams reshuffled reality: suddenly Dr Dent was treating Billy Jr. Dreams had always been central to Burroughs's work, and he catches them very evocatively. Places are transfigured and blended, with 'narrow sloping streets of vaguely Parisian cast', a city 'vaguely reminiscent of New York', and Piccadilly Circus backing on to a maze of narrow, twisted, Arab-style streets. His dreams were inhabited by people he had once known, in a personal Land of the Dead – his parents, Gysin, Sommerville, Kiki, Antony Balch – with the characteristic dream porosity of inner and outer, like a Delvaux painting ('The usual mixture of rooms and squares and streets that is the mark of the Land of the Dead. Streets lead into kitchens and bedrooms, so no area is completely private or completely public'; 'there is no line between streets and private house'.[47])

There was a similar porosity between dreaming and waking itself. If a man could visit Paradise in a dream, Coleridge once said, and take a flower as proof that he had been there, and if he found it in his hand on waking: 'What then?'[48] When Burroughs asked Victor Bockris how he would define the difference between dream and reality, Bockris said you didn't have a bruise in the morning if someone hit you in a dream. 'Oh don't you?' said Burroughs; 'That's not true at all, my dear. I've woken up with a black eye.'[49] It is playful, but his extreme Romanticism in relation to the dream world underscores his relation to Surrealism, so obvious as to go largely unmentioned (although the curator of his late art retrospective *Ports of Entry*, Robert A. Sobieszek, described him as 'primarily a surrealist'[50]).

Appearing in 1995, *My Education* was Burroughs's last book in his lifetime, not long before his multimedia career was further consecrated by the Ports of Entry show in 1996. Burroughs had never gone out of fashion, building and building since the 1960s, and his celebrity was now immense. 'All young people need some-body bad to look up to', John Waters has said (talking about himself); 'Sort of a filth elder, if you will.'

Burroughs in Lawrence with artworks, in a 1987 photograph by Philip Heying.

For his last couple of decades Burroughs was the Filth Elder par excellence, and the effect was enhanced by his paradoxically conservative demeanour. Over and above his extraordinary vision of personal freedom, his weird integrity and his distinctly American brand of anti-Americanism, his loveable badness was commodified for a large audience through readings and recordings. 'He asked me what the American Flag means to me', drawls the octogenarian Burroughs, 'and I said "Soak it in heroin Doc, and I'll suck it!"'[51] He had cameo roles in films, collaborated with rock and hip-hop groups, sang the old Marlene Dietrich number 'Falling in Love Again', and – in one of his more noteworthy late projects – wrote the libretto for an opera with Tom Waits, *The Black Rider*. He even appeared, notoriously, in an advert for Nike training shoes, doffing his hat at the end. There was something unashamedly vaudevillian about his late persona.

One of the late Burroughs's harshest critics was American writer Dennis Cooper. Burroughs's late work was just dabbling at his former craft, after he had been repackaged, sometime around the 1970s, 'as a kind of outlaw comedian / philosopher' and the Burroughs mystique – with the guns, the heroin, the crazy beliefs in aliens and CIA conspiracies – was just 'showbiz'. In fact for Cooper, Burroughs was 'essentially an active relic who had exploited the mystique around his early work for so long that I suspect he didn't even know why he was famous anymore.'[52]

Back home in his small Kansas town Burroughs was seen, in the words of James Grauerholz, as 'a cherished old gink'.[53] Burroughs was well cared for by Grauerholz and a roster of volunteers who cooked for him, drove him around, and generally looked after his needs. On a typical day Burroughs would take his methadone before eating breakfast, and by the afternoon he might be practising with handguns or throwing knives, before settling down to read gun magazines or pulp fiction. He could also browse his collection of books about death, such as *Sudden and Awful*, *Weird Ways to Die*, *How Did They Die Vols 1 & 2*, and *They Went That-Away*.

Burroughs abhorred daytime drinking but drank solidly in the evenings. In the 1970s this had meant 6 p.m. onwards, but in old age the hour of the sundowner crept forward to 3.30 p.m., when he would have some vodka and Coke and perhaps smoke a joint; he was a steady, lifelong cannabis smoker and associated it with his creativity (despite his earlier 1940s perception that 'tea heads' tended to be 'silly' and 'paranoiac'[54]). He might then do a little writing in his journal, but he had to conserve his energy and often napped in the afternoons. Friends would come for dinner, and then he tended to make an early night, turning in around nine with his .38 snubnose under the bedclothes in case of intruders.

Burroughs was frail, bald and stooped, but he was alive and largely alert. When interviewers remarked on his age he attributed it to healthy living. He had never been lonely, he once said, because he had his fictional characters, and now in old age he had the companionship of his friends and his cats (or his 'familiars,' as he saw them[55]). With age and narcotics, sex was no longer much of an issue – although there is a remarkable and authentic account published on the internet by a seventeen- or eighteen-year-old youth who sought him out[56] – but Burroughs still took pleasure in food, and the art that covered his walls. This was mostly by himself and Gysin, and he also had a picture by Ralph Steadman of Edwardian-looking men sailing around the sky in balloons and flying machines: he liked this, he said in 1996, because it 'exudes an odd nostalgia for the future'.[57]

Gysin was gone, of course, and so were Joan and Kells Elvins and Kiki and Ian Sommerville and Antony Balch. It is only appropriate that in the Kansas years Burroughs, in his cups, would sometimes sing to himself the Mexican tango song 'Adios Muchachos'[58] (' . . . Companeros de mi Vida . . .')[59] Later in life he had a new wave of bereavements and outlivings, notably Ginsberg, who died in April 1997. Huncke, Leary and Terry Southern had died the year before. Burroughs was also hit hard by the deaths of the cats he felt had taught him so much. One by one they died and were buried around the pond in the garden: the last to go was Fletch, in July 1997.

It had been a long, strange, unforeseen journey for the most unpopular boy in St Louis, but now it was coming to an end. On Friday 1 August 1997 Tom Peschio, one of Burroughs's younger friends and assistants, arrived to fix dinner and found him having chest pains. Peschio was alarmed, perhaps more alarmed than Burroughs, and after he called an ambulance Burroughs told him everything was all right. To the best of Peschio's memory, Burroughs said something like 'It's OK, I'll be right back' (now the title – *I'll Be Right Back*, mixed media, 2004 – of a Damien Hirst artwork about him). 'I think he just said it to reassure me,' says Peschio, 'which was weird that he'd reassure me.'[60]

Burroughs lost consciousness and died the following day at Lawrence Memorial Hospital, aged 83, without saying anything further. His last written words seem to have been scrawled in his journal on Wednesday 30 July:

Love? What is it?
Most natural painkiller what there is.
LOVE.[61]

References

1 St Louis Blues

1 William S. Burroughs, *Junky* (London, 1977), p. xi.
2 *Naked Lunch: The Restored Text* (London, 2005), p. 210. Ellipsis in original.
3 See David T. Courtwright, *Dark Paradise: Opiate Addiction in America Before 1940* (Cambridge, MA, 1982).
4 1985 interview with David Ohle in *My Kind of Angel: I.m. William Burroughs*, ed. Rupert Loydell (Exeter, 1998), p. 33.
5 Ibid., p. 27.
6 Laura Lee Burroughs, *Homes and Flowers: Refreshing Arrangements*, vol. III (Atlanta, GA, 1942), pp. 56; 58.
7 'Introduction: A Passport for William Burroughs', in Victor Bockris, *A Report from the Bunker with William Burroughs* (London, 1982), p. xiv.
8 Burroughs in *My Kind of Angel*, ed. Loydell, p. 30.
9 Cited in Ted Morgan, *Literary Outlaw: The Life and Times of William S. Burroughs* (London, 1991), p. 24.
10 Cited in ibid., p. 30, and later to provide a chapter heading in *The Wild Boys* (London, 1972), p. 32.
11 Ibid.
12 See 'Word', *Interzone* (London, 1990), pp. 66–8, and letter to Ginsberg, 24 July 1958, *The Letters of William S. Burroughs 1945–1959*, ed. Oliver Harris (London, 1993) p. 393.
13 Morgan, *Literary Outlaw*, p. 31.
14 'Lee's Journals', in *Interzone* (London, 1990), p. 117.
15 'St Louis Return', in *The Burroughs File* (San Francisco, 1984), p. 83.
16 Ibid., p. 88, further playing on the fact that this arcade later burned down.

17 Letter to Allen Ginsberg, 18 May 1959, in *The Letters of William S. Burroughs 1945–1959*, ed. Oliver Harris (London, 1993), p. 415.

18 *Cobble Stone Gardens* (Cherry Valley, NY, 1976), p. 10.

19 'The Driving Lesson', *Interzone*, p. 18.

20 'St Louis Return', p. 81.

21 Ibid.

22 Insults often remembered late in life, e.g. *The Place of Dead Roads* (London, 1984) p. 17; *Exterminator!* (New York, 1973), p. 10.

23 Heard by present writer, London 1982, cf. e.g. journal entry of 28 December 1997, *Last Words* (London, 2000), p. 33.

24 *The Wild Boys* (London, 1972), p. 32.

25 Cited Morgan, *Literary Outlaw*, p. 36.

26 Ibid., pp. 33–4.

27 Burroughs in *My Kind of Angel*, ed. Loydell, p. 34.

28 Cited Morgan, *Literary Outlaw*, p. 45.

29 Cited in ibid., p. 48.

30 Ibid., p. 43.

31 Cited in ibid., p. 51.

32 *The Yage Letters* (San Francisco, 1981), p. 11.

33 Cited Morgan, *Literary Outlaw*, p. 52.

34 Burroughs, *Junky*, p. xii.

35 'The Name is Burroughs', *The Adding Machine* (London, 1985), p. 2.

36 Ibid., p. 2; heard by the present writer in London, 1982; see 'The Lemon Kid', *Exterminator!* (New York, 1973), p. 9.

37 Lord Cheshire and Reggie recalled in 'The Name is Burroughs', p. 7; 'The Junky's Christmas' [1954] in *The Junky's Christmas and Other Stories* (London, 1994), 'The "Priest", They Called Him' [1967] in *Exterminator!*, quotation from p. 159.

38 'The Name is Burroughs', p. 3.

39 Ibid.

40 The whole text is reproduced in *Word Virus: The William S. Burroughs Reader*, ed. James Grauerholz and Ira Silverberg (New York, 1998), p. 23.

41 Jack Black, *You Can't Win* (New York, 1926), p. v.

42 William Burroughs, 'Foreword', Jack Black, *You Can't Win* (New York, 2000), p. 11.

43 Black, *You Can't Win* (1926), p. 162.

44 Burroughs, 'Foreword', *You Can't Win*, p. 12.

2 The Hidden Antagonist

1 *Junky* (London, 1977), p. xiii.
2 See *My Education: A Book of Dreams* (London, 1995), p. 7.
3 'Sredni Vashtar', *The Penguin Complete Saki* (London, 1982), p. 136. Further quotes pp. 138, 139.
4 Burroughs in conversation with Christopher Isherwood, 1975, in *Burroughs Live: The Collected Interviews of William S. Burroughs, 1960–1997* (New York, 2001), ed. Sylvère Lotringer, p. 369.
5 Rupert Loydell, ed., *My Kind of Angel: I.m. William Burroughs* (Exeter, 1998), p. 20.
6 *Times Literary Supplement*, 5 December 1929, p. 970.
7 *The Wild Party* by Joseph Moncure March with drawings by Art Spiegelman (New York, 1994), p. vi.
8 'Twilight's Last Gleamings', *Interzone* (New York, 1989), pp. 3–12.
9 'The Name is Burroughs', *The Adding Machine* (London, 1985), p. 9.
10 Too screwy; act of collaboration: ibid.
11 1970 interview in *Burroughs Live*, ed. Lotringer, p. 159.
12 1987 interview in ibid., p. 680.
13 Cited James Campbell, *This Is The Beat Generation* (London, 1999), p. 24.
14 1972 interview in *Burroughs Live*, ed. Lotringer, p. 166.
15 Cited in Ted Morgan, *Literary Outlaw: The Life and Times of William S. Burroughs* (London, 1991), p. 73.
16 1978 interview in *Burroughs Live*, ed. Lotringer, p. 411.
17 *Junky*, p. xiv.
18 *My Education*, p. 145.
19 *Junky*, p. 72.
20 Ibid.
21 'The Finger', *Interzone*, p. 15.
22 Ibid., p. 17.
23 'Dream of the Penal Colony', *Interzone*, p. 45.
24 'The Finger', p. 17.
25 Peter Swales, *New York Observer*, 24 May 1993.
26 1981 interview in *Burroughs Live*, ed. Lotringer, p. 538.
27 Cited Morgan, *Literary Outlaw*, p. 80.
28 Samuel Beckett, *Proust* (London, 1965), p. 55.

29 William Burroughs, 'Beckett and Proust', *The Adding Machine* (London, 1985), p. 184.

30 Ibid., p. 185.

31 Barry Miles, *William Burroughs: El Hombre Invisible* (London, 1992), p. 31.

32 *Exterminator!* (New York, 1973), p. 3. Subsequent quotations p. 8. It is possible that Burroughs's depiction of himself shouting in the street is an artistic reworking.

3 New York, New York

1 James Campbell, *The Beat Generation* (London, 1999), p. 23.

2 Jack Kerouac, *The Vanity of Duluoz* (London, 1969), pp. 217–18. Ginsberg features as Irwin Garden.

3 Ibid., p. 211.

4 *The Letters of William S. Burroughs 1945–1959*, ed. Oliver Harris (London, 1993), pp. 128; 68.

5 Kerouac, *The Vanity of Duluoz*, p. 208.

6 Ibid., p. 230.

7 Cited Morgan, *Literary Outlaw*, p. 107.

8 'First Recordings', *The Third Mind* (London, 1979), p. 89.

9 'Hippos', from extract reproduced in *Word Virus: The William S. Burroughs Reader*, ed. James Grauerholz and Ira Silverberg (New York, 1998), pp. 30; 33.

10 'Remembering Jack Kerouac', *Adding Machine*, p. 179.

11 'Gangsterling', cited by James Grauerholz, *Word Virus*, p. 11.

12 'Nice Old Gentleman', *My Education: A Book of Dreams* (London, 1995), p. 145; hysterics and paranoids, 'On Freud and the Unconscious', *The Adding Machine* (London, 1985), p. 89.

13 Cited Barry Miles, *Ginsberg* (New York, 1989), p. 96.

14 *Interzone* (New York, 1989), p. 123.

15 *The Soft Machine* (London, 1968), p. 160.

16 *The Western Lands* (New York, 1988), p. 201.

17 Burroughs, *The Letters of William S. Burroughs 1945–1959*, ed. Oliver Harris (London, 1993), p. 115.

18 *Queer* (New York, 1985), p. 16.

19 Barry Miles, *William Burroughs: El Hombre Invisible* (London, 1992), p. 38.

20 Ibid.

21 Kerouac, *The Vanity of Duluoz*, p. 215.

22 Cited Miles, *Hombre Invisible*, p. 37.

23 Huncke, *The Evening Sun Turned Crimson* (New York, 1980), p. 111.

24 See 'God's Own Medicine', *The Adding Machine*, p. 107.

25 Edward St Aubyn, *Bad News* (London, 1992), p. 48.

26 John Jones, *The Mysteries of Opium Reveal'd* (London, 1701), p. 29.

27 'I Am Dying, Meester?', *Yage Letters Redux*, ed. Oliver Harris
    (San Francisco, 2006), p. 76.

28 Thomas De Quincey, *Confessions of an English Opium-Eater*
    (London, 1822), pp. 94–7.

29 *Junky* (London, 1977), p. 7.

30 Ibid., p. 7.

31 Huncke, *Evening Sun Turned Crimson*, p. 111.

32 *Junky*, p. xvi.

33 Ibid., p. 5.

34 Huncke, *Evening Sun Turned Crimson*, p. 111.

35 *Junky*, p. 13.

36 Ibid., pp. 41–2.

37 *Naked Lunch: The Restored Text* (London, 2005), p. 5.

38 1965 interview in *Burroughs Live: The Collected Interviews of William
    S. Burroughs, 1960–1997*, ed. Sylvère Lotringer (New York, 2001), p. 72.

39 Ibid.

40 Kerouac, *The Vanity of Duluoz*, pp. 269–70.

41 Burroughs, *The Letters of William S. Burroughs 1945–1959*, ed. Oliver
    Harris (New York, 1993), p. 83.

42 Cited in Harris, 'Introduction' to *The Yage Letters Redux*, pp. xxv–xxvi.

43 *Junky*, p. 7.

44 Ibid., pp. 125–6.

45 Ann Marlowe, *How to Stop Time: An A–Z of Heroin* (New York, 1999),
    p. 9.

46 Eric Detzer, *Monkey on my Back* (London, 1990), p. 106.

47 *Junky*, p. 15.

48 Ibid., p. 27.

49 *Letters*, pp. 91; 98.

50 Morgan, *Literary Outlaw*, p. 128.

4 Go South, Young Man

1 *Junky* (London, 1977), p. 110.
2 Barry Miles, *William Burroughs: El Hombre Invisible* (London, 1992), p. 43; Ted Morgan, *Literary Outlaw: The Life and Times of William S. Burroughs* (London, 1991), pp. 136–7.
3 *The Yage Letters*, with Allen Ginsberg (San Francisco, 1963), pp. 37; 47.
4 *The Letters of William S. Burroughs 1945–1959*, ed. Oliver Harris (New York, 1993), p. 51.
5 Jack Kerouac, *On The Road* (London, 1958), p. 152.
6 Ballard, 'Sticking To His Guns', *The Guardian*, 24 August 1993.
7 *Letters*, pp. 8, 22, 23.
8 Ibid., pp. 66, 29, 25.
9 Ibid., pp. 58, 43, 57, 58.
10 Ibid., p. 51.
11 *Junky*, p. 16.
12 *Letters*, p. 27.
13 Ibid., p. 38.
14 Ibid., p. 43.
15 Ibid., p. 63.
16 *Junky*, p. 114.
17 *Letters*, pp. 65, 78; *Soft Machine* (London, 1968), p. 13.
18 *Letters*, pp. 61, 69.
19 *Junky*, p. 130.
20 *Letters*, p. 79.
21 Ibid., pp. 89–90.
22 *Junky*, p. 111.
23 James Grauerholz, 'The Death of Joan Vollmer Burroughs: What Really Happened?', at http://old.lawrence.com/burroughs/deathofjoan, pp. 23; 4.
24 Account from Morgan, *Literary Outlaw*, p. 177.
25 *Letters*, p. 68.
26 *Junky*, p. 152.
27 *The Yage Letters*, p. 5.
28 Dominic Streatfield, *Brainwash: The Secret History of Mind Control* (London, 2006), pp. 81–2.
29 Alan Ansen, *William Burroughs* (Sudbury, MA, 1986), p. 13.

30 *Queer* (New York, 1985), pp. 50–51; 95.

31 Ibid., p. 96.

32 *Everything Lost: The Latin American Notebook of William S. Burroughs*,
     ed. Oliver Harris (Columbus, OH, 2008), p. 129.

33 Letter to Ginsberg of 4 June 1952; *Letters*, p. 128.

34 *Letters*, pp. 132–3.

5 A Slip of the Gun

1 *The Yage Letters*, with Allen Ginsberg (San Francisco, 1963), p. 14; *Queer*
     (New York, 1985), p. 91; *Everything Lost: The Latin American Notebook of
     William S. Burroughs*, ed. Oliver Harris (Columbus, OH, 2008), p. 181.

2 Eddie Woods to Ted Morgan in Ted Morgan, *Literary Outlaw: The Life
     and Times of William S. Burroughs* (London, 1991), p. 196.

3 James Campbell, *This Is The Beat Generation* (London, 1999), pp. 120–21.

4 Woods in James Grauerholz, 'The Death of Joan Vollmer Burroughs:
     What Really Happened?', at
     http://old.lawrence.com/burroughs/deathofjoan, p. 34.

5 William Burroughs, 'My Most Unforgettable Character', in Michael
     Spann, *William Burroughs' Unforgettable Characters* (Brisbane, 2001),
     p. 54.

6 Morgan, *Literary Outlaw*, p. 200.

7 William S. Burroughs Jr, *Kentucky Ham* (New York, 1973), p. 31.

8 Ibid.

9 'Dream Record: June 8, 1953' in Allen Ginsberg, *Reality Sandwiches*
     (San Francisco, 1963), p. 48.

10 *The Letters of William S. Burroughs 1945–1959*, ed. Oliver Harris
     (New York, 1993), p. 263.

11 *Minutes of the Vienna Psychoanalytic Society*, 10 April 1907 (New York,
     1962), p. 65.

12 *Last Words: The Final Journals of William Burroughs* (London, 2000),
     p. 17.

13 Burroughs, 'Introduction' [1985] to *Queer*, p. 18.

14 *Junky* (London, 1977), p. 112.

15 Cited Morgan, *Literary Outlaw*, p. 205.

16 *Letters*, pp. 119–20.

17 Cited Harris, *Yage Letters Redux* (San Francisco, 2006), p. xxxv.

18 *Yage Letters*, pp. 8–9.

19 Burroughs, 'Yage Article', Appendix 5 of *Yage Letters Redux*, p. 91.

20 *Letters*, p. 166.

21 *Yage Letters Redux*: Halliday, p. xix; Burroughs, p. 29.

22 Ibid., pp. 44–5.

23 Description of yagé state collated from real letter to Ginsberg of 8 July 1953, *Letters*; fictionalized letter to Ginsberg of 'July 10th 1953', *The Yage Letters*, pp. 50–53; 'Notes from yagé state' in 'The Market' section of *Naked Lunch: The Restored Text* (London, 2005) pp. 91–2.

24 *Letters*, p. 181.

25 Ibid., pp. 171; 179; 180.

26 Ibid., p. 290.

27 *Everything Lost*, p. 187.

28 Perse, *Winds* [*Vents* 1946, trans. 1953] (New York, 1961) pp. 115; 73; 77; *Anabasis* [1924, trans. 1930] (London, 1959), p. 35.

29 *Naked Lunch*, p. 92.

30 Information in Ginsberg's caption to photograph of 1 September 1953; Ginsberg Deposit.

31 *The Yage Letters*, pp. 50–53, ellipses mine.

32 *Everything Lost*, p. 187, slightly normalized.

33 Ibid., pp. 183; 185; 193.

34 Ibid., p. 129.

35 *Everything Lost*, pp. 189; 209; 185.

36 Cited Morgan, *Literary Outlaw*, p. 209.

37 *Burroughs Live: The Collected Interviews of William S. Burroughs, 1960–1997* (New York, 2001), ed. Sylvère Lotringer, p. 807.

38 Miles, *Hombre Invisible*, p. 59.

39 Morgan, *Literary Outlaw*, p. 230.

40 Cited Miles, *Hombre Invisible*, pp. 58; 59; 59; 59.

41 Alan Ansen, *William Burroughs* (Sudbury, MA, 1986), p. 4.

42 Ansen enclosure in Burroughs's letter to Ginsberg, 2 January 1954, *Letters*, p. 194.

6 Tangier and *Naked Lunch*

1 'International Zone', *Interzone* (London, 1990), p. 59.

2 Cited in Iain Finlayson, *Tangier* (London, 1992), p. 93.

3 *Interzone*, p. 58, cf. *The Letters of William S. Burroughs 1945–1959*, ed. Oliver Harris (London, 1993), p. 330.

4 Ibid., p. 205.

5 Ibid., pp. 222, 226, 213.

6 Ibid., p. 204.

7 Ibid., p. 206.

8 *Interzone*, pp. 66, 50, 70.

9 *Letters*, pp. 266.

10 Ibid., pp. 224, 223.

11 Ibid., pp. 303, 216; *Interzone*, pp. 74–5.

12 Ted Morgan, *Literary Outlaw: The Life and Times of William S. Burroughs* (London, 1991), p. 241.

13 *Interzone*, p. 50

14 *Letters*, p. 326.

15 Marie-Jacqueline Lancaster, *Brian Howard: Portrait of a Failure* (London, 1968), p. 430.

16 Letter to John Banting, circa March 1954, in *Brian Howard*, ed. Lancaster, pp. 529–30.

17 *Letters*, p. 204.

18 Ibid., p. 215.

19 Ibid., pp. 217, 310.

20 Ibid., p. 216; cf. *Interzone*, p. 127.

21 *Letters*, pp. 260, 262.

22 'Lee's Journals', *Interzone*, p. 69.

23 *Letters*, p. 266; cf. pp. 268–9.

24 'The Conspiracy', *Interzone*, pp. 108–9.

25 *The Place of Dead Roads* (London, 1984), p. 42.

26 'The Name is Burroughs', *The Adding Machine* (London, 1985), p. 11.

27 *The Soft Machine* [1961] (London, 1968), p. 185.

28 Letter to John Montgomery, 23 February 1959, currently in possession of Andrew Sclanders, London.

29 *Letters*, p. 380.

30 Cited Morgan, *Literary Outlaw*, p. 259.

31 'Graham Greene', *The Adding Machine*, p. 187.

32 *Letters*, p. 326.

33 Gerald Richardson, *Crime Zone* (London, 1959), pp. 162–3.

34 *Letters*, p. 326.

35 Kerouac, *Desolation Angels* (London, 1966), p. 311.

36 Gerald Nicosia, *Memory Babe: A Critical Biography of Jack Kerouac* (New York, 1983), p. 545.

37 *Letters*, pp. 345, 337.

38 Bowles, 'Burroughs in Tangier', *The Burroughs File* (San Francisco, 1984), p. 15.

39 'Burroughs in Tangier', *The Burroughs File*, p. 16.

40 *Letters*, p. 346 n. 49.

41 Ibid., pp. 365, 375.

42 Ibid., p. 365.

43 *Naked Lunch: The Restored Text* (London, 2005), p. 188.

44 Letter of 7 December 1985, *In Touch: The Letters of Paul Bowles* (London, 1994), p. 526.

45 Burroughs cited Miles, *Hombre Invisible*, p. 87.

46 *Letters*, p. 298.

47 *Naked Lunch*, p. 173.

48 *Letters*, p. 266.

49 Ibid., p. 215.

50 Ibid., p. 289.

51 Ibid., pp. 378, 411.

52 Ibid., p. 359.

53 Ibid., p. 385.

7 Paris: Cut-ups at the Beat Hotel

1 Barry Miles, *The Beat Hotel* (London, 2001), p. 69.

2 Ginsberg to Orlovsky, cited in *The Letters of William S. Burroughs 1945–1959*, ed. Oliver Harris (London, 1993), p. 386, n. 4.

3 Miles, *The Beat Hotel*, p. 76.

4 Cited ibid., p. 71.

5 Jeremy Mercer, *Books, Baguettes and Bedbugs* (London, 2006), p. 75.

6 'Paris Please Stay the Same', *The Adding Machine* (London, 1985), p. 104.

7 Ibid., pp. 104–5.
8 *Letters*, p. 386.
9 Cited Miles, *The Beat Hotel*, p. 78.
10 Both cited James Campbell, *This Is The Beat Generation* (London, 1999), p. 223; the juxtaposition is Campbell's.
11 Ted Morgan, *Literary Outlaw: The Life and Times of William S. Burroughs* (London, 1991), p. 291.
12 Letter from Kerouac on Celine, *Paris Review* (Winter / Spring 1964).
13 Los Angeles . . . Jeeews . . . Celine novel . . . pond . . . definitively aside: Burroughs in conversation with Victor Bockris, *A Report from the Bunker* (London, 1982), pp. 15–16.
14 'Interesting person'; 'nice person', *Letters*, pp. 389; 393.
15 Ibid., pp. 416–17.
16 Introduction to *The Last Museum* (New York, 1986) and elsewhere.
17 Cited in Michelle Greene, *The Dream At The End of The World* (London, 1992), p. 78
18 Salvador Dalí, *Diary of a Genius* (London, 1994), p. 189.
19 Burroughs in 1960 dialogue with Gysin, reprinted in Gysin and Wilson, *Here to Go* (London, 1985), pp. 173 / 175.
20 'Cut-Ups: A Project for Disastrous Success' [1964], reproduced Brion Gysin, *Back in No Time: The Brion Gysin Reader*, ed. Jason Weiss (Middletown, CT, 2001), p 130.
21 *Letters*, p. 398; Chinese painter story cited in Morgan, *Literary Outlaw*, p. 482.
22 Gysin, *Back in No Time*, p. 122.
23 'C-U: APFDS', *Back in No Time*, p. 130.
24 Letter to present writer from Terry Wilson, April 2001.
25 Morgan, *Literary Outlaw*, p. 235.
26 *Letters*, pp. 398–9; 398.
27 Ibid., p. 396.
28 Ibid., p. 415.
29 He served five and wrote a book, *The Total Beast*, about his experience.
30 *Letters*, p. 405.
31 Ibid., pp. 405; 419; cf. Morgan, *Literary Outlaw*, pp. 306ff.
32 *Letters*, p. 411.
33 Ibid., p. 411.
34 Death, worlds, no going back: ibid., pp. 415; 420; 411.

35 'C-U: APFDS', *Back in No Time*, ed. Weiss, p. 125.

36 *Letters*, p. 406.

37 1985 interview with David Ohle in *My Kind of Angel: I.m. William Burroughs*, ed. Rupert Loydell (Exeter, 1998), p. 27.

38 'Paris Please Stay The Same', *The Adding Machine* (London, 1985), p. 105.

39 Morgan, *Literary Outlaw*, p. 314.

40 Cited in ibid., p. 316.

41 Cited Miles, *The Beat Hotel*, p. 185.

42 Cited Barry Miles, *William Burroughs: El Hombre Invisible* (London, 1992), p. 103.

43 Static handshake, creepy kicks; cited Miles, *The Beat Hotel*, pp. 185; 187.

44 Cited Miles, *The Beat Hotel*, p. 193.

45 Letter cited Morgan, *Literary Outlaw*, p. 320.

46 'I am Dying, Meester?' (1963), *Yage Letters Redux* (San Francisco, 2006) p.78.

47 Cited Morgan, *Literary Outlaw*, p. 361.

48 Cited ibid., p. 323.

49 Interview with Joseph Barry in *New York Post* [1963], reproduced in *Burroughs Live*: Beckett, p. 49; Burroughs, p. 50.

50 'Precise Intersection Points', *Third Mind*, with Brion Gysin (London, 1979), p. 136.

51 Preface [1985] to *Queer* (New York, 1985), pp. 16; 15; 15.

52 *Letters*, p. 431. The joke is identified in Oliver Harris's notes.

53 Ibid., pp. 430; 434.

8 Burroughs 1960–65: Undesirable Alien

1 According to Gysin, in 'Cut-Ups: A Project for Disastrous Success', *The Third Mind* (London, 1979), p. 44.

2 Cyril Connolly, *The Unquiet Grave* (London, 1945), p. 62.

3 Cited in John Geiger, *Chapel of Extreme Experience: A Short History of Stroboscopic Light and the Dream Machine* (New York, 2003), p. 10.

4 Ibid., pp. 24; 54–5.

5 Ibid., p. 66.

6 Paul Bowles, letter of 12 December 1964, *In Touch: The Letters of Paul Bowles* (London, 1994), p. 370.

7 Cited Geiger, *Chapel of Extreme Experience*, p. 53.

8 *Letters of Aldous Huxley*, ed. James Sexton (Chicago, 2007), p. 475.

9 Cited Ted Morgan, *Literary Outlaw: The Life and Times of William S. Burroughs* (London, 1991), p. 367.

10 Cited ibid., p. 368.

11 Geoffrey Gorer, *Bali and Angkor* (London, 1936), Appendix I, 'Mescaline', pp. 214–17, ellipses mine.

12 Morgan, *Literary Outlaw*, p. 369.

13 Cited ibid., p. 377.

14 Timothy Leary, *High Priest* (New York, 1968) p. 219.

15 Ibid., pp. 215; 218–19.

16 Timothy Leary, 'Programmed Communication During Experiences with DMT', *Psychedelic Review*, 8 (1966).

17 Morgan, *Literary Outlaw*, pp. 381; 382.

18 Cited ibid., p. 382.

19 Leary, *High Priest*, p. 216.

20 Journal entry, March 1959, in Joseph Cornell, *Theatre of the Mind: Selected Diaries, Letters and Files*, ed. Mary Ann Caws (London, 1993), p. 254.

21 'Beckett and Proust', *The Adding Machine* (London, 1985), p. 185.

22 Interviewed by Conrad Knickerbocker, *Paris Review*, 35 (Fall 1965); reprinted in *Burroughs Live: The Collected Interviews of William S. Burroughs, 1960–1997*, ed. Sylvère Lotringer (New York, 2001), p. 65.

23 Jean Cocteau, *Opium* [1930] (London, 1968), p. 145.

24 'It Belongs to the Cucumbers', *The Adding Machine*, p. 53.

25 E.g. in his Naropa lecture on cut-ups, Track 2 of CD *First Thought, Best Thought*.

26 'Fold-ins', *The Third Mind*, p. 95, earlier in *Transatlantic Review*, 11 (London, 1962).

27 Cited Morgan, *Literary Outlaw*, p. 340.

28 Cited by John Calder in his foreword to *The Naked Lunch: A New Edition Containing the 'Ugh' Correspondence* (London, 1982).

29 *Times Literary Supplement*, 14 November 1963.

30 Michael B. Goodman and Lemuel Coley, *William S. Burroughs: A Reference Guide* (New York, 1990), p. 218.

31 'Academy 23', *The Job* (London, 1970), p. 136.

32 1982 interview, *Burroughs Live*, ed. Lotringer, p. 551.

33 'Mr Bradley-Mr Martin is two people because it is a statement of the impasse of [the] dualistic universe which he has created'; 1965 interview, *Burroughs Live*, ed. Lotringer, p. 95.

34 1965 interview, *Burroughs Live*, ed. Lotringer, p. 83.

35 *Yage Letters Redux*, p. 71.

36 *Nova Express* (London, 1966), pp. 13–14.

37 *The Soft Machine* (London, 1968), appendix, p. 172.

38 Tony Tanner, *City of Words: American Fiction 1950–1970* (London, 1971), p. 133.

39 *Burroughs Live*, ed. Lotringer, p. 606.

40 Cited Morgan, *Literary Outlaw*, p. 401.

41 Barry Miles, 'A Checklist of the Books of William Seward Burroughs', *Final Academy* (London, 1982), p. 37.

42 Cited Morgan, *Literary Outlaw*, p. 402.

43 *Times Literary Supplement*, Letters section, 2 January 1964.

44 Burroughs in Victor Bockris, *With William Burroughs: A Report from the Bunker* (London, 1982), p. 74.

45 Anthony Burgess, *Enderby Outside* (London, 1968), p. 138.

46 *Naked Lunch: The Restored Text* (London, 2005), pp. 129; 169.

47 *Times Literary Supplement*, 6 August 1964, pp. 682–3.

48 *Interzone* (London, 1990), p. 130.

49 Burroughs, 'Foreword' to Joe Maynard and Barry Miles, *William S. Burroughs: A Bibliography* (Charlottesville, VA, 1978), p. xi.

50 'St Louis Return', *The Burroughs File* (San Francisco, 1984), pp. 83; 89; 83.

51 'Last Awning Flaps on the Pier', in ibid., p. 134.

52 In *Architectural Design*, XXXIX/6 (June 1969), p. 314.

53 *Back in No Time: The Brion Gysin Reader*, ed. Jason Weiss (Middletown, CT, 2001), p. 3.

54 Burroughs letter to Peter Matson, 8 March 1973, in possession of present writer.

55 Carl Weissner, in Bockris, *With William Burroughs*, p. 8.

56 Barry Miles, notes to 1995 CD re-issue.

57 Cited Morgan, *Literary Outlaw*, p. 420.

9 Swinging London, 1966–73

1 'Conversations: Genesis P. Orridge and Charles Kemp', *New Style* magazine, 10 (1978), p. 15.

2 Barry Miles, *William Burroughs: El Hombre Invisible* (London, 1992), p. 148. Hampton Court, Ted Morgan, *Literary Outlaw: The Life and Times of William S. Burroughs* (London, 1991), p. 429.

3 Robert Anton Wilson, *Cosmic Trigger* (Scottsdale, AZ, 1991), pp. 43–5.

4 Cited Morgan, *Literary Outlaw*, p. 372.

5 Burroughs's thoughts on the insect trust – as in *Naked Lunch: The Restored Text*, p. 123 – gave rise to the title of the small press poetry magazine, *The Insect Trust Gazette*, which first appeared in Summer 1964 and featured work by Burroughs and Gysin among others.

6 Ginsberg in Miles, *Hombre Invisible*, p. 119; Miles in Victor Bockris, *With William Burroughs: A Report from the Bunker* (London, 1982), p. 47.

7 Gysin and Wilson, *Here to Go* (London, 1985), pp. 219, 227, 228.

8 Gysin to present writer, 2 October 1982.

9 As paraphrased in Morgan, *Literary Outlaw*, p. 440. Rock C. Slam, ibid., p. 441.

10 Currently in possession of Andrew Sclanders, London.

11 Control addict cited Miles, *Hombre Invisible*, p. 155; resenting his perfection cited Morgan, *Literary Outlaw*, p.442.

12 Reprinted in *Burroughs Live: The Collected Interviews of William S. Burroughs, 1960–1997*, ed. Sylvère Lotringer (New York, 2001); quotations from pp. 104; 105; 111; 109.

13 *International Times*, no. 119 (16–30 December 1971): centrefold.

14 To Claude Pelieu and Mary Beach, 10 December 1969, formerly in possession of Andrew Sclanders, London.

15 Cited Morgan, *Literary Outlaw*, p. 565.

16 Cited ibid., p. 456.

17 See ibid., pp. 454–5, Bockris, *With William Burroughs*, pp. 120–21. Morgan says 1972, Burroughs in Bockris says 1971.

18 Brion Gysin, 'The Pipes of Pan', first published in 1964 in Ira Cohen's journal *Gnaoua*, and subsequently reprinted as liner notes for the LP record *Brian Jones Presents the Pipes of Pan* (1971).

19 Andrew Sclanders, *Beat Books* catalogue 48, item 173.

20 Cited Morgan, *Literary Outlaw*, p. 407.

21 Burroughs to Lou Reed, Bockris, *With William Burroughs*, p. 25.

22 *The Place of Dead Roads* (New York, 1983), pp. 171; 176.

23 *The Western Lands* (New York, 1988), p. 252.

24 'Playback from Eden to Watergate', later version in *The Job*, revised and enlarged edition (New York, 1974).

10 Holding the Bunker

1 Victor Bockris, *With William Burroughs: A Report from the Bunker* (London, 1982), p. 83.

2 'It Belongs to the Cucumbers', *The Adding Machine* (London, 1985), pp. 53–4.

3 *Fanatic No.2: Special Low Mindedness Issue* (Amsterdam, 1976) [two page spread, unpaginated]

4 Ted Morgan, *Literary Outlaw: The Life and Times of William S. Burroughs* (London, 1991), p. 303.

5 Ibid., pp. 491; 492.

6 Christmas Humphreys, *A Popular Dictionary of Buddhism* (New York, 1962), p. 140.

7 Bockris, *With William Burroughs*, p. 204.

8 Ibid., pp. 91; ix.

9 Ibid., pp. 155; 148; 153.

10 Morgan, *Literary Outlaw*, p. 541; it has been suggested Stern was talking to the dial tone.

11 Bockris, *With William Burroughs*, pp. 87; 58.

12 Ibid., p. 117.

13 See *Desolation Angels* (New York, 1995), p. 341.

14 Bockris, *With William Burroughs*, p. 199.

15 Ibid., pp. 181; 189.

16 Brion Gysin to present writer, 2 October 1982.

17 See Bockris, *With William Burroughs*, pp. 138–43.

18 Bockris, *With William Burroughs*, p. 163.

19 Khem Caigan, 'From Necronomicon to Pazuzu and Whirlwinds', in *Kaos*, 14, ed. Joel Birocco (London, 2002), p. 83.

20 Cited Morgan, *Literary Outlaw*, p. 563.

21 Cited ibid., p. 528.

22 Edmund White, 'The Inner Burroughs: This Is Not A Mammal',
   reprinted *Burroughs Live: The Collected Interviews of William S. Burroughs,
   1960–1997*, ed. Sylvère Lotringer (New York, 2001), pp. 473–9. Sontag
   is identified in Edmund White, *City Boy* (London, 2010), p. 242.
   Quotations pp. 473; 475.
23 Ibid., p. 477.
24 Cited Morgan, *Literary Outlaw*, p. 564.

11 Kansas 1981–97: Adiós Muchachos

1 Cited Ted Morgan, *Literary Outlaw: The Life and Times of William
   S. Burroughs* (London, 1991), p. 571.
2 Duncan Fallowell, 'Fast Frames Slow Draw', *Time Out*, 24–30 September
   1982, p. 12.
3 *Last Words* (London, 2000), p. 186.
4 See ibid., pp. 97; 213.
5 'Contact'; 'cat charade', *The Cat Inside* (New York, 1986), p. 70.
6 Cited Morgan, *Literary Outlaw*, p. 606.
7 *The Cat Inside*, p. 6.
8 *Burroughs Live: The Collected Interviews of William S. Burroughs, 1960–1997*,
   ed. Sylvère Lotringer (New York, 2001), p. 645.
9 *The Western Lands* (New York, 1988), p. 248.
10 *Naked Lunch* (London, 2005), p. 92. See also 'A Distant Thank You'
   section of *Nova Express*, with 'the lemur people' imagined as all
   gentleness and emotional feeling, without any aggression.
11 *Last Words*, p. 216.
12 *Burroughs Live*, p. 497.
13 Ibid., p. 497.
14 Ginsberg wrote a short piece commemorating him that October,
   published in Fainlight's posthumous *Selected Poems* (London, 1986).
   Barry Miles has confirmed to the present writer that Burroughs knew
   of Fainlight's death.
15 *Dead Roads*, pp. 285–6.
16 See, for example, 'MOB', *New Edinburgh Review* (Summer 1979), p. 40.
17 *The Drug User: Documents 1840–1960*, ed. D. Strausbaugh and D. Blaise
   (New York, 1991), foreword by Burroughs.

18 *Dead Roads*, p. 217.

19 *The Western Lands*, p. 203.

20 Ibid. p. 252.

21 'Statement on the Final Academy', *The Final Academy* (London, 1982).

22 Morgan, *Literary Outlaw*, p. 9.

23 Cited by Burroughs in his introduction to *The Last Museum* (reprinted in Brion Gysin, *Back in No Time: The Brion Gysin Reader*, ed. Jason Weiss (Middletown, CT, 2001) pp. xiii–xiv).

24 Introduction to *The Last Museum*.

25 Cited Morgan, *Literary Outlaw*, p. 613.

26 Cited by Sylvère Lotringer, *Burroughs Live*, p. 650.

27 *My Education*, p. 147; cf. *The Cat Inside*, p. 78.

28 *New Yorker*, 11 August 1980.

29 Horovitz in *My Kind of Angel: I.m. William Burroughs*, ed. Rupert Loydell (Exeter, 1998), p. 62.

30 *The Cat Inside*, p. 49. Seemingly from Verlaine's *Sagesse*, where the poet, with his *âme veuve* ('widowed soul') reviews the past, 'comme un mauvais fleuve!'. Burroughs attributes it to Verlaine in his late journals, *Last Words* (London, 2000), p. 67.

31 *Burroughs Live*, p. 798.

32 Ibid., p. 758; Loydell, ed., *My Kind of Angel*, p. 32.

33 Trance state to CIA; Burroughs and Ginsberg in conversation, *Burroughs Live*, pp. 813–14.

34 'I like the shaman' cited Miles, *Hombre Invisible*, p. 223. Persona, Wolberg, better than psychoanalysis; Burroughs and Ginsberg in conversation, *Burroughs Live*, pp. 814–15.

35 See *Last Words*, pp. 147–55.

36 Ibid., p. 72.

37 Morgan, *Literary Outlaw*, p. 591.

38 'Civilian Defence', *The Adding Machine* (London, 1985), p. 82.

39 *Magick in Theory and Practice*, ed. John Symonds and Kenneth Grant (London, 1973), pp. 214–15.

40 *Burroughs Live*, p. 758.

41 Stine, 'Symbolic Machines' and 'The Symbolic Hieronymous Machine' in *On the Frontiers of Science* (New York, 1985), pp. 60–94; Campbell, 'Addendum on the Symbolic Psionic Machine' in *Astounding Science Fiction*, LIX/4 (June 1957), modifying his earlier pieces 'Psionic Machine

– Type One', ASF, LVII/4 (June 1956), and 'Correction and Further Data on the Hieronymous Machine', ASF, LVII/6 (August 1956).

42 *Burroughs Live*, p. 475.

43 See *Naked Lunch* (London, 2005), pp. 92–3.

44 1981 interview, *Burroughs Live*, p. 571; cf. 1984 interview, *Burroughs Live*, p. 610; Burroughs himself makes a point about going 'full circle' back to the magical universe in *My Education*, p. 156.

45 See *OED* entry for 'maggot': Noun 1; sense 2a.

46 Richard Dawkins, quoting N. K. Humphrey in *The Selfish Gene* (London, 1978), pp. 206–7.

47 *My Education*: old time junkies p. 171; Dent treating Billy p. 44; places pp. 40, 177, 30; inner/outer porosity pp. 34, 37.

48 *The Notebooks of Samuel Taylor Coleridge*, ed. Kathleen Coburn (New York and London, 1957–2002), vol. III, n. 4287.

49 Victor Bockris, *With William Burroughs: A Report from the Bunker* (London, 1982), p. 204.

50 Robert A. Sobieszek, *Ports of Entry: William S. Burroughs and the Arts* (Los Angeles, 1996), p. 25.

51 A line which always went down well in performance, from 'The Do-Rights'; an old Burroughs piece in *Mayfair*.

52 Dennis Cooper, *All Ears: Cultural Criticism Essays and Obituaries* (New York, 1999), pp. 144, 145, 143.

53 Cited in 'The Inner Circle: Memories Collected from the FOBS (Friends of Burroughs)' by Frank Tankard, currently available on the internet at www.lawrence.com/news.2007/jul/30/inner_circle.

54 *Junky* (London, 1977), pp. 17–18.

55 See e.g. *The Cat Inside*, p. 67.

56 'In Bed with Burroughs' by Marcus Ewert, available on the internet: www.lawrence.com/news/2007/jul/30/bed_burroughs.

57 *Burroughs Live*, p. 778.

58 Mimi Thebo to present writer, 30 September 2008.

59 'Goodbye, Friends' (' . . .Companeros of my life . . .')

60 Tankard, 'The Inner Circle'.

61 *Last Words*, p. 253.

Select Bibliography

Works by Burroughs

[As William Lee] *Junkie: Confessions of an Unredeemed Drug Addict*
    (New York, 1953)
The Naked Lunch (Paris, 1959)
Minutes to Go, with Brion Gysin, Sinclair Beiles, Gregory Corso (Paris, 1960)
The Exterminator, with Brion Gysin (San Francisco, 1960)
The Soft Machine (Paris, 1961)
'Comments on the Night Before Thinking', *Evergreen Review*, 5
    (September–October 1961)
The Ticket That Exploded (Paris, 1962)
Dead Fingers Talk (London, 1963)
The Yage Letters, with Allen Ginsberg (San Francisco, 1963)
Roosevelt After Inauguration (New York, 1964)
Nova Express (New York, 1964)
'The Literary Techniques of Lady Sutton-Smith', *Times Literary Supplement*
    (6 August 1964)
Time (New York, 1965)
APO-33 Bulletin: A Metabolic Regulator (San Francisco, 1966)
So Who Owns Death TV?, with Claude Pelieu and Carl Weissner
    (San Francisco, 1967)
The Dead Star (San Francisco, 1969)
'St Peter's Building (1888)', *Architectural Design*, xxxix/36 (June 1969)
The Job (New York, 1970)
The Last Words of Dutch Schultz (London, 1970)
'The Revised Boy Scout Manual' [as three cassettes, 1970], printed in
    RE-Search 4-5: William S. Burroughs, Brion Gysin, and Throbbing Gristle

(San Francisco, 1982)

Ali's Smile (Brighton, 1971)

The Wild Boys (New York, 1971)

Electronic Revolution (Cambridge, 1971)

Exterminator! (New York, 1973)

White Subway (Brighton, 1973)

Mayfair Acadamy [sic] *Series, More or Less* (Brighton, 1973)

Port of Saints (London, 1973)

'Face to Face with the Goat God', *Oui* magazine (August 1973)

Snack (London, 1975)

The Last Words of Dutch Schultz [film script] (New York, 1975)

The Book of Breeething with Bob Gale (Ingatestone, 1975)

Cobble Stone Gardens (New York, 1976)

The Retreat Diaries (New York, 1976)

Junky (New York, 1977)

The Third Mind, with Brion Gysin (New York, 1978)

Blade Runner: A Movie (Berkeley, CA, 1979)

Ah Pook is Here (London, 1979)

Port of Saints (Berkeley, CA, 1980)

Early Routines (Santa Barbara, CA, 1981)

Cities of the Red Night (New York, 1981)

'Introduction: God's Own Medicine', in Dean Latimer and Jeff Goldberg,
    Flowers in the Blood: The Story of Opium (New York, 1981)

The Place of Dead Roads (New York, 1983)

The Burroughs File (San Francisco, 1984)

'Foreword to BEAT HOTEL', in Harold Chapman, *The Beat Hotel*
    (Geneva, 1984)

Queer (New York, 1985)

The Adding Machine (London, 1985)

The Cat Inside (New York, 1986)

'Preface' to Brion Gysin, *The Last Museum* (New York, 1986)

The Western Lands (New York, 1988)

'Foreword' to Jack Black, *You Can't Win* (New York, 1988)

Interzone (New York, 1989)

Ghost of Chance (New York, 1991)

'Foreword' to John Strausbaugh and Donald Blaise, eds, *The Drug User:
    Documents 1840–1960* (New York, 1991)

Painting and Guns (New York and Madras, 1992)

'Introduction' to *Everything is Permitted: The Making of 'Naked Lunch'*,
    ed. Ira Silverberg (London, 1992)

The Letters of William S. Burroughs 1945–1959, ed. Oliver Harris (New York,
    1993)

'Voices in Your Head', introduction to John Giorno, *You Got to Burn to
    Shine* (London, 1994)

Foreword to Denton Welch, *In Youth is Pleasure* (Cambridge, MA, 1994)

My Education: A Book of Dreams (New York, 1995)

Word Virus: The William S. Burroughs Reader, ed. James Grauerholz and
    Ira Silverberg (New York, 1998)

Last Words: The Final Journals of William S. Burroughs, ed. James
    Grauerholz (New York, 2000)

'My Most Unforgettable Character', in Michael Spann, *William Burroughs'
    Unforgettable Characters* (Brisbane, 2001)

Naked Lunch: The Restored Text, ed. James Grauerholz and Barry Miles
    (New York, 2003)

The Yage Letters Redux, ed. Oliver Harris (San Francisco, 2006)

Everything Lost: The Latin American Notebook of William S. Burroughs,
    ed. Oliver Harris (Columbus, OH, 2008)

Bibliography

Collaborative, epistolary, extensively variant, minor, underground:
Burroughs's bibliography is exceptionally complex, but he has been well
served by his bibliographers.

Miles Associates [Barry Miles], *A Descriptive Catalogue of the William
    S. Burroughs Archive* (London, 1973)

Maynard, Joe, and Barry Miles, *William S. Burroughs: A Bibliography
    1953–1973* (Charlottesville, VA, 1978)

Miles, Barry, 'A Checklist of the Books of William Seward Burroughs',
    in *The Final Academy* (London, 1982)

Sinclair, Iain, 'Kerouac, Burroughs, Ginsberg, The Definitive Catalogue:
    [Part 1] Wm. Seward Burroughs', in *Driffs: The Antiquarian and Second
    Hand Book Fortnightly*, no. 1 (8–22 January 1986)

Goodman, Michael B., and Lemuel Coley, *William S. Burroughs: A Reference Guide* (New York, 1990)

Shoaf, Eric C., *Collecting William S. Burroughs in Print* (Rumford, RI, 2000)

Biography, Interviews, Criticism

Ansen, Alan, *William Burroughs: An Essay* (Sudbury, MA, 1986)

Bockris, Victor, *A Report from the Bunker with William Burroughs* (London, 1982)

Campbell, James, *This is the Beat Generation* (London, 1999)

Chapman, Harold, *The Beat Hotel* (Geneva, 1984)

Cooper, Dennis, 'King Junk', in *All Ears: Cultural Criticism, Essays and Obituaries* (New York, 1999)

The Final Academy: Statements of a Kind (London, 1982)

Grauerholz, James W., 'The Death of Joan Vollmer Burroughs: What Really Happened?', at http://old.lawrence.com/burroughs/deathofjoan

Harris, Oliver, *William Burroughs and the Secret of Fascination* (Carbondale, IL, 2003)

Hibbard, Allen, ed., *Conversations with William S. Burroughs* (Jackson, FL, 1999)

Lotringer, Sylvère, ed., *Burroughs Live: The Collected Interviews of William S. Burroughs, 1960–1997* (New York, 2001)

Loydell, Rupert, ed. *My Kind Of Angel: i.m. William Burroughs* (Exeter, 1998)

Lydenberg, Robin, *Word Cultures* (Chicago, 1987)

Miles, Barry, *William Burroughs: El Hombre Invisible* (London, 1992)

—, *The Beat Hotel* (London, 2001)

Morgan, Ted, *Literary Outlaw* (London, 1991)

Mottram, Eric, *William Burroughs: The Algebra of Need* (London, 1977)

Murphy, Timothy S., *Wising Up the Marks: The Amodern William Burroughs* (Berkeley, 1997)

RE-Search 4-5: William S Burroughs, Brion Gysin, and Throbbing Gristle (San Francisco, 1982)

Review of Contemporary Fiction: William S. Burroughs Number (Spring 1984)

Russell, Jamie, *Queer Burroughs* (Basingstoke, 2001)

Schneiderman, Davis, and Philip Walsh, *Retaking the Universe: William S. Burroughs in the Age of Globalisation* (London, 2004)

Skerl, Jennie, *William S. Burroughs* (Boston, MA, 1985)
—, and Robin Lydenberg, eds, *William S. Burroughs: At the Front: Critical Reception, 1959–1989* (Carbondale, IL, 1991)
Sobieszek, Robert A., *Ports of Entry: William S. Burroughs and the Arts* (Los Angeles, 1996)
Tankard, Frank, 'The Inner Circle: Memories Collected from the FOBS (Friends of Burroughs)', at
    www.lawrence.com/news.2007/jul/30/inner_circle
Tanner, Tony, *City of Words: American Fiction 1950–1970* (London, 1971)
Weissner, Carl, *Burroughs: Eine Bild-Biographie* (Berlin, 1994)

Acknowledgements

Everyone working on Burroughs owes a debt to Ted Morgan, Burroughs's first biographer. I had reservations about his book when it first appeared, but I have since come to respect it as a heroic feat of research and an indispensable work of reference.

More personally, I'd like to thank Peter Hale of the Ginsberg Trust for going the extra mile in overcoming illustration problems; Oliver Harris, not only for his invaluable work in extending the Burroughs canon but for finding time to cast an eye over the present book, and for his unfailing Burrovian cordiality; and Andrew Sclanders of Beat Books for his enthusiasm, expertise, and generosity in sharing rare material.

I'm also grateful to Mark Allen, David Barrett, James Campbell, Antony Clayton, Philip Heying, George Laughead, Ian MacFadyen, Barry Miles, Jim Pennington, Mark Pilkington, Ian Pindar, Bill Redwood, Gavin Semple, Paul Sieveking, Mimi Thebo, and Carl Williams. Johnsons all. Writing came at a difficult time and I'd never have got through it without Sheena Joughin. This book is for her.

Photo Acknowledgements

The author and publishers wish to express their thanks to the following sources of illustrative material and/or permission to reproduce it.

Beat Books, Andrew Sclanders: pp. 9, 12, 58, 66, 94, 119, 126, 127, 148, 151, 153, 156, 157, 160, 191; photo Victor Bockris: p. 177; photo Harold Chapman: p. 122; © DACS 2010: p. 76; photo Simon Dell: p. 150; Getty Images: pp. 123, 128, 145; photos Allen Ginsberg: pp. 41, 78, 82, 87, 100; The Ginsberg Trust: pp. 41, 74, 78, 82, 87, 100; photo Philip Heying: p. 195; Landau Fine Art, Montreal: p. 76; Los Alamos Historical Museum Photo Archives: p. 15; photo by Barry Miles: p. 164; Jim Pennington: p. 6; Paul Sieveking: p. 173; Topfoto: p. 122.